*The
Millionaire's
Book of
Quotations*

The Millionaire's Book of Quotations

MARK FISHER

Thorsons
An Imprint of HarperCollinsPublishers

Thorsons.
An Imprint of HarperCollins*Publishers*
77—85 Fulham Palace Road,
Hammersmith, London W6 8JB

Published by Thorsons 1991
10 9 8 7 6 5 4 3 2 1

A CIP catalogue record for this book
is available from the British Library.

ISBN 0-7225-2499-4

Typeset by Harper Phototypesetters Limited,
Northampton, England
Printed in Great Britain by
Mackays of Chatham, Kent

Contents

Preface

When I was still a young man, I was lucky enough to encounter a book entitled *The Road To Happiness* by Dr Victor Pauchet. The preface states: 'Health, success and happiness are acquired by re-educating yourself.' That's all it took to fire up my enthusiasm. In fact, Victor Pauchet — who is simply repeating Socrates' famous phrase 'know thyself' 2000 years later — has transformed the lives of thousands of people and inspired hundreds of authors, my humble self included. Which goes to show just how much influence a book can have on an individual's life.

Take Victor Pauchet's positive philosophy, and add to it the great principles formulated by men and women who have achieved exceptional success, such as John Rockefeller, J. Paul Getty, Howard Hughes, Vanderbilt, Estée Lauder, etc., and you have *The Millionaire's Book of Quotations*. I firmly believe that books such as these not only penetrate the mysteries of financial achievement, but also provide us with the keys to happiness and self-fulfilment. And isn't that what we're all ultimately striving for?

During my career as a financial advisor, I often had occasion to call upon the guidelines, principles and secrets collected in this book. I feel the quotations herein will be of great help to anyone determined to embark on the road to success, as well as a constant source of inspiration, motivation and encouragement to all those striving to reach the summit in their chosen field, whatever it may be.

Charles Albert Poissant C.A.

Introduction

Do you have a seemingly unsolvable problem that you can't work out yourself? Well, why not consult with Baron Rothschild, Harold Geneen (President of ITT for more than 20 years), Howard Hughes, Sam Goldwyn, Thomas J. Watson Sr (founder of IBM), Malcolm Forbes, and hundreds of others well known and not so well known, all of them members in good standing of the Millionaire's Club?

HOW ONE IDEA — AND ONLY ONE — CAN MAKE YOU RICH!

In business, the arts, literature, commerce — in all fields without exception — an idea can be worth a million dollars. In fact, anyone who has succeeded in business and built a large fortune knows that it all starts with one idea. An idea that might have seemed crazy to everyone else — colleagues, relatives, friends and associates alike. The illustrious and wealthy people whose thoughts fill these pages have had just these kinds of crazy ideas, which were met with scepticism and derision by their peers until they were proven to work.

You might be asking yourself how to hire the right person, how better to sell or persuade people, how to delegate and get more out of your time. You might be on the verge of throwing in the towel because of some obstacle or error, or because you're afraid to lose out on a deal. The people quoted in this book will become your personal advisors, like full-time members of your new 'board of directors'. They don't have to be with you physically. What you need from them is the fruit of their long experience, their thoughts and advice, and that's exactly what you'll find here.

Of course a book can't make decisions for you, but it can help you considerably. The wisdom and experience on which our contributors' advice is based represent a fantastic source of motivation. Many of those quoted had to overcome difficult beginnings, with no one to support them, no money behind them, and often no education to back them up. All they had was the burning desire to get rich and succeed, just like you and me!

All great individuals — and there's one in each of us just waiting for the opportunity to embark on the road to success — had models they could admire and emulate. *The Millionaire's Book of Quotations* will provide you with the models you need.

HOW CAN YOU PUT THIS GOLD-MINE TO GOOD USE?

You can open this unique book at any page and be certain to encounter concepts which will have a positive influence on your mind and push you toward the summit of success, whether you're looking for lucrative ideas and infallible formulas to start a business, or for ways to motivate your sales team, or material for a speech or article, or to add a humorous twist to that business letter. Let the rich and outstanding be your guides.

The advice offered is not theoretical. It was not developed by academics with no firsthand experience, or by self-styled 'experts'. Every word is the direct result of hands-on experience on the part of people who have put their ideas into practice and proved their worth. Isaac Newton said, 'If I rose so high, it's because I stood on the shoulders of giants.' He was referring to the sages of antiquity, whose writings he studied, and who inspired him to make the discovery that changed the face of the entire world. By reading this book, you can also climb onto the shoulders of the ancients. And not only sages of the distant past, but more recent ones as well—the best kept secrets of living millionaires, some of who are still under fifty years old.

There are a thousand-and-one ways to read the book. You can start at the beginning and read through to the end without stopping. Or you can pause to meditate and admire the gems of wisdom being imparted to you. You can also stop to have a good laugh. Almost every page offers some humorous advice, tempered only by its pertinence, practicality and depth. There's a reason behind this: most people whose thoughts and philosophies are included here have been endowed with — or more likely developed — a great sense of humour.

Or you can open the book at random, when you have a few minutes to spare. Maybe you're not looking for a great way to make money, or for some guiding principle to help you in business. Maybe you just need to read a quotation by someone you admire, or for whom you feel an affinity. All you have to do is consult the appendix, where you will find fuller information on the key figures quoted.

GREAT MINDS THINK ALIKE

What is interesting about *The Millionaire's Book of Quotations* is that the contributors come from such a wide variety of professions; from real estate to mechanics, electronics, publishing, cinema, retail sales, oil, food products, finance, the stock exchange, hotels, restaurants etc. You will find there are similarities in the search for success, no matter the field.

This is the case because one thing is certain: success is in no way the result of luck alone. That is, of course luck plays a role. But as Louis Pasteur said, 'luck sprouts in fertile ground.' Gary Player put it another way: 'The harder you work, the luckier you get!'

If you study the lives, philosophies and works of these great individuals, you realize that they were all very scientific in the application of precise principles that led to their success. Not surprising, really, yet I am always astonished to see that most people — at least those who are not rich and are not on the road to becoming rich — believe that fortunes are made because of some kind of magic spell, effortlessly, and without any conception of the indispensable 'millionaire's mentality' which crops up in so many variations.

THE TIMELESS SECRET OF WEALTH LIES HIDDEN IN THESE PAGES!

Is there a sure-fire formula for getting rich? A secret that would allow anyone — despite lack of education, experience, contacts or money — to transform his or her dreams into material gain? Or is wealth the exclusive privilege of a small minority?

The good news is that the infallible secret does exist, and it is contained in these pages. All the wealthy people I have had the privilege of knowing personally — as well as those whose lives I have studied — applied this secret, of which all other principles of success are variations, results or corollaries. It appears countless times, formulated in many different ways, within this book. Telling you it straight out would be too easy — only when you are ready — that is when your desire to get richer and improve all aspects of your life is sincere — and if you are attentive, which you must be in order to take advantage of the golden opportunity being offered here, you will discover the 'secret of secrets'.

The Millionaire's Book of Quotations will undoubtedly become one of your favourite reference books, because it offers not only a philosophy of wealth but also a complete philosophy of life. For you will find that most very rich individuals were — or became — philosophers: It was this profound understanding of the universal and eternal laws of life and humanity that enabled them to get so far so fast.

In any field, success comes more easily — and more quickly — when you know how to get what you want. These pages contain all the advice you need on how to make money and achieve success. So don't miss the opportunity. You too can make your dreams a reality! Today is the first day of the rest of your life. It doesn't matter what you've done up to now, or what failures you've faced in the past, or what experience you're lacking. If in your heart you have the desire to make a fortune — and I know that secretly it's there, like a fragile yet tenacious flame — then you will succeed, thanks to *The Millionaire's Book of Quotations* and your new 'colleagues and advisors!'

A

ABUNDANCE

When riches come, they come so quickly, in such great abundance, that one wonders where they have been hiding during all those lean years.

Napoleon Hill

Consider the lilies of the field, how they grow; they toil not, neither do they spin. And yet I say unto you, that even Solomon in all his glory was not arrayed like one of these.

Matthew VI:28

ACCOUNTANTS
See also Accounting.

I don't need any bodyguards, but what I do need are a couple of expertly trained accountants.

Elvis Presley

Accountants and lawyers make great accountants and lawyers. We need them, but we make the business decisions.

Estée Lauder

ACCOUNTING
See also Bankers; Banks.

[My philosophy is] discipline, order, and faithful account of all credits and debits.

John Rockefeller

Accounting is a malicious extension of the banking conspiracy.

Henry Ford

ACHIEVEMENT

From where you sit, you can probably reach out with comparative ease and touch a life of serenity and peace. You can wait for things to happen and not get too sad when they don't. That's fine for some but not for me. Serenity is pleasant, but it lacks the ecstasy of achievement.

Estée Lauder

ACQUISITION

Never acquire a business you don't know how to run.

Robert W. Johnson

ACTION

No one knows what he can do till he tries.

Publius Syrus

He who wants, but doesn't act, is a pest.

William Blake

Discussion is the fruit of many men, action the fruit of one.

Charles de Gaulle

The superior man acts before speaking, and then speaks in accordance with his actions.

Confucius

When in doubt, jump!

Malcolm Forbes

In any financial operation, one should act before anyone has the chance to react.

Baron Philippe de Rothschild

Business affairs are not very sensitive. They rely on everyday activities, and must be decided each day.

Montesquieu

Even if the prospects seem bad, you have to carry on. Continuing to hold back could be even more dangerous.

General Eisenhower

Action should not be confused with haste.

Lee Iacocca

Once a decision has been made and all that's left is to carry it out, then all apprehension about the final result must be deliberately put aside. Which means this: as soon as you've made a reasonable decision, based on factual information, the time has come for action.

Nolan Bushnell

In any undertaking, two-thirds depends on reason, one-third on chance. Increase the first fraction and you are faint-hearted. Increase the second and you are foolhardy.

Napoleon

Actions speak louder than words.

Dale Carnegie

Never put off for tomorrow what you can do today.

Benjamin Franklin

Action creates more fortunes than prudence.

Marquis de Vauvenargues

I see myself as a doer. I'm sure that other people have had ideas that were similar to mine. The difference is that I have carried mine into action, and they have not.

Nolan Bushnell

You can't think and hit the ball at the same time.

Lawrence Peter 'Yogi' Berra

ADVANCEMENT

In any organization men should move up from the bottom to the top. That develops loyalty, ambition and talent, because there is a chance for promotion. Never inject a man into the top, if it can be avoided. In a big organization, to have to do that, I think, is a reflection on management. Of course there are always exceptional cases.

Alfred P. Sloan

What good does it do to look back? Business is business. The world belongs to the living!

Helena Rubinstein

ADVERSITY
See also Bad Times; Defeat; Failure; Struggle.

Every adversity, every failure and every heartache carries with it the Seed of an equivalent or a greater Benefit.

Napoleon Hill

A period of continuous bad luck is as improbable as always staying on the straight path of virtue. In both cases, there will eventually be a curve.

Charles Chaplin

The ideal man is not only nourished by adversity, but goes out of his way to seek out difficulties and obstacles.

Friedrich Nietzsche

ADVERTISING

Advertising Agency: eighty-five percent confusion and fifteen percent commission.

Fred Allen

Doing business without advertising is like winking at a girl in the dark: you know what you're doing, but nobody else does.

Stewart Henderson Britt

Advertising may be described as the science of arresting human intelligence long enough to get money from it.

Stephen Leacock

A promise, such a promise — that is the soul of any ad.

Samuel Johnson

Publicity is the greatest art form of the 20th Century.

Marshall McLuhan

Advertising should enhance the scenery. It has to be popular and beautiful at the same time.

Jacky Setton

Kodak sells film, but they do not advertise film. They advertise memories.

Theodore Levitt

Half the money I spend on advertising is wasted, but the trouble is I don't know which half.

John Wanamaker

Many a small thing has been made large by the right kind of advertising.

Mark Twain

The most important word in the vocabulary of advertising is TEST. If you pretest your product with consumers, and pretest your advertising, you will do well in the marketplace.

David Ogilvy

Advertise your objective, don't keep it in the dark. Whatever your occupation, whatever you propose doing, if you need the support of the public then take the steps necessary to let them know about it. It doesn't matter how, as long as you get their attention. I frankly admit that I owe a large part of my success to the press. Some businessmen will say that their advertising costs are a complete waste of money. That may be, but it's because the ads were done carelessly and parsimoniously. Small doses of advertising result in nothing, obviously. It's like giving a sick person half the medicine he needs. It just causes more suffering. Give the whole dose, and the cure will be certain and decisive.

P.T. Barnum

You often hear people say they don't have the means to advertise. They're wrong — what they're lacking is the means not to advertise. In a country where everyone reads the newspaper, you have to be pretty thick-headed not to understand that the press is the best and cheapest medium to communicate with the public.

Businessmen in general do not appreciate the system of newspaper advertising. It's the surest way to success. But you need nerve and faith to try it. Nerve because you have to throw a gold brick into the uncertain waters of the future, and faith because there will be many difficult days before you will see the returns start rolling in, all because of some well-placed ink on a few sheets of paper.

P.T. Barnum

Those who are absent or remain silent are always wrong. To assure successful promotion, you have to be present, daily, in order to create it.

Bernard Tapie

You can have the most wonderful product in the world, but if people don't know about it, it's not going to be worth much. There are singers in the world with voices as good as Frank Sinatra's, but they're singing in their garages because no one has ever heard of them. You need to generate interest, and you need to create excitement.

Donald Trump

ADVISORS

The correct behaviour for an advisor is to question everything, produce nothing, and talk at the right time.

Thomas Jefferson

Executive advisors are people who borrow your watch to tell you the time, and then don't give it back.

Robert Townsend

AGE

At seventy four I sold, for the sum of two million dollars, my fried chicken business, which I'd started at the age of sixty five, when I was getting ready to live out my days on social security.

Colonel Sanders

Take away all the men over fifty, and the world would stop turning.

Henry Ford

People are always amazed by the fact that I didn't start McDonald's before I was 52 years old, and that I was an overnight success. But I was just like so many people in the entertainment business who practice their routine for years with hardly any notice, and then suddenly find themselves in the spotlight of stardom. I did achieve success from one day to the next, that's true, but my 30 years of preparation were like a long, long night!

Ray Kroc

AGREEMENT
See also Advisors.

I don't want a bunch of yes-men around me. I want people to tell me the truth — even if it costs them their job.

Samuel Goldwyn

When someone says that they agree with an idea On Principle, it means that they don't have the slightest intention of carrying it out.

Otto von Bismarck

ALIMONY

You never realize how short a month is until you pay alimony.

John Barrymore

AMBITION
See also Mentality.

You direct a garage or a business like you drive a bus. It does its round, stopping to pick people up, but it can't make a long distance trip. Of course you can be happy driving the same route all your life. But I wanted to drive bigger and faster buses, and see other places.

Soichiro Honda

The first one gets the oyster, the second gets the shell.

Andrew Carnegie

I refuse failure, and I never give up.

Régine

I'm here to make a fortune!

Coco Chanel

ANTICIPATION

We should always be prepared for the worst.

Georges Hatsopoulos

APPEARANCES
See also Clothes; Complexes; Efficiency.

Nothing succeeds like the appearance of success.

Christopher Lascl

It seems like yesterday that a young applicant asked a partner of Clarkson Gordon if, once hired, he should cut off his beard. The answer was: 'Not at all, my boy, as long as you don't wear it between 9 and 5.'

Peter C. Newman

ARDOUR
See also Enthusiasm; Passion; Zeal.

Whatever you do, do it ardently. If necessary, get used to getting up early and going to bed late. Never leave any stone unturned. And if you only have one hour to work with, make sure that what you do in that hour is perfectly done. The old proverb makes a lot of sense: 'What is worth doing is worth doing well.' Energy and patience in business are two indispensable elements of success.

P.T. Barnum

ARGUMENT

When your argument has little or no substance, abuse your opponent.

Cicero

ASKING
See also Audacity.

Asking only costs a moment of embarrassment. Not asking means being embarrassed your whole life.

Japanese proverb

ASSOCIATES

Men take on the nature, the habits and the power of thought of those with whom they associate in a spirit of sympathy and harmony.

Napoleon Hill

The man who goes alone can start today; but he who travels with another must wait till that other is ready.

Henry David Thoreau

ATTACK

A great advantage in business is knowing when to take the offensive: the person under attack always comes to terms.

Benjamin Constant

AUDACITY

To succeed in this world, remember these three maxims: to see is to know; to desire is to be able to; to dare is to have.

Alfred de Musset

Tact in audacity is knowing just how far is too much.

Jean Cocteau

Fortune does not favour the sensitive among us: it smiles on the audacious, who are not afraid to say — 'The die is cast.'

Erasmus

Fortune smiles on the audacious.

Virgil

The boundary between the impossible and the extraordinary is extremely fine; life is a promise of adventure, often extraordinary, never impossible. Passion and fantasy can certainly result in excess, but if you have to choose between excess and immobility, don't hesitate. Always and everywhere you have to dare.

Bernard Tapie

AUTHORITY

Nothing demonstrates authority better than silence.

Charles de Gaulle

I never shout. I don't threaten. I make promises and I deliver.

Helene Martini

When in charge, meditate. When in doubt, mumble. When in difficulty, delegate.

Anonymous

AWARDS

Awards are like hemorrhoids; in the end, every asshole gets one.

Frederick Raphael

B

BACHELORS

Rich bachelors should be heavily taxed. It's not fair that some men should be happier than others.

Oscar Wilde

BAD TIMES
See also Adversity; Crisis; Defeat; Failure; Struggle.

These times, like all times, are very good ones, if we but know what to do with them.

Ralph Waldo Emerson

There is no such thing as bad times, I kept telling myself. There is no such thing as bad business. Business is there if you go after it.

Estée Lauder

It's when things are going badly that you should build. Why wait for things to pick up, and for everything to cost more?

Ray Kroc

BANKERS
See also Banks.

A banker is a person who is willing to make a loan if you present sufficient evidence to show you don't need it.

Herbert V. Prochnow

A good banker, unfortunately, is not someone who anticipates danger and avoids it. He is rather a person who ruins himself and all his colleagues in an orthodox and conventional way, by not admitting that he is at fault.

John Maynard Keynes

A banker is someone who lends you his umbrella when the sun is shining, and takes it back when it starts to rain.

Mark Twain

If you want time to pass quickly, just give a banker your note for 90 days.

J.P. Morgan

Banking is a career from which no one recovers.

John Kenneth Galbraith

BANKS
See also Bankers.

Banking establishments are more dangerous than marching armies.

Thomas Jefferson

I was too expensive for the banks. That's why I had to count on myself.

Samuel Goldwyn

It's the workshop that has to finance an industrial enterprise, and not the bank. For me, a bank is above all a secure and convenient place to keep money in reserve, and I think it's better if the bank serves my interests, rather than my serving theirs.

Henry Ford

BEGINNINGS

The beginning is the most important part of the work.

Horace

He has half the deed done, who has made a beginning.

Horace

BEING
See also Being Yourself; Character; Depending on Yourself.

One must be something in order to do something.

Goethe

BEING RIGHT

No one can be right all of the time, but it helps to be right most of the time.

Robert Half

Always be sure you're right — then go ahead.

Davy Crockett

BEING YOURSELF
See also Character; Depending on Yourself.

Cultivate what the public does not like about you, that is who you are.

Jean Cocteau

You cannot achieve great success until you are faithful to yourself.

Friedrich Nietzsche

Anyone who thinks they are not a genius has no talent.

Edmond Goncourt

BENEFACTORS

The men who create productivity, opportunity, employment, wealth and wages for a community are public benefactors and should be recognized as such.

William Randolph Hearst

BENEVOLENCE

Benevolence is invincible if it is sincere, without pretension and hypocrisy.

Marcus Aurelius

BILLIONAIRES
See also Millionaires.

If you can calculate how much you have, then you are not a billionaire!

John Paul Getty

BORROWING
See also Bankers; Banks.

If you're short, take a loan. Never ask for a small amount.
Ask for what you need, and always pay it back, the sooner
the better.

Aristotle Onassis

Behind every millionaire hides a frenzied borrower.

Aristotle Onassis

That was the only amount I ever borrowed. But I never
regretted it. And I was able to pay it back with interest a
few months later.

Helena Rubinstein

BOSSES
See also Authority.

Asking who should be the boss is like asking who should
play saxophone in a quartet — obviously the one who
knows how to play.

Henry Ford

I learned that a boss doesn't just give orders, but also, and
most importantly, sets an example. He or she has to know
how to make others better, and show them what to do. He
nourishes them on what Shakespeare called 'the milk
of human kindness', as well as with the energy necessary
to win.

Bernard Tapie

I started out by giving myself a salary of one dollar a year. Those who command have to set an example. But if you really feel like the boss, you will be followed step for step. The employees won't become exactly like you, but almost. And when the boss speaks, everyone listens; when the boss acts, everyone watches; they are attentive to his every move.

Lee Iacocca

If you think your boss is stupid, remember: you wouldn't have a job if he was any smarter.

Albert A. Grant

BUREAUCRACY

The only thing that saves us from bureaucracy is its inefficiency.

Eugene McCarthy

BUSINESS

Business is business.

George Coleman

BUYING
See also Credit; Selling.

I have enough money to last me the rest of my life, unless I buy something.

Jackie Mason

Whoever said money can't buy happiness didn't know where to shop.

Anonymous

There are certainly a great many things that money can't buy, but it's funny: have you ever tried to buy them without money?

Ogden Nash

A study of economics usually reveals that the best time to buy anything is last year.

Marty Allen

C

CALM

Remember that everything is only opinion, and that opinions depend on you. So suppress your opinions, and like a ship that's rounded the cape, you will find yourself in calm water, the raging sea subsided, floating on gentle waves.

Marcus Aurelius

CAPITAL

The man going into business for himself also needs sufficient capital, but this is the least important factor. Just as a bad workman invariably complains that he has bad tools, so the bad businessman always wails that he does not have enough capital.

John Paul Getty

I am convinced that the more money a new business needs to begin with, the less chance it has of being a success.

Mark McCormark

There is no intrinsic reason for the scarcity of capital.

John Maynard Keynes

My capital belongs to me, it's my head and I would never be stupid enough to let someone cut it off.

Bernard Tapie

CAPITALISM

What is the difference between capitalism and communism? Capitalism is the exploitation of man by man; communism is the reverse.

Polish joke

It [the first McDonald's restaurant] was only the first step in my struggle to build a personal monument to capitalism.

Ray Kroc

CARS

If you stay in Beverly Hills too long you become a Mercedes.

Robert Redford

CHALLENGE

Making money represents the same challenge for a businessperson as breaking records does for an athlete.

Bernard Tapie

The most delicate challenge we have to face in the eighties is to make sure our business remains an interesting place to work.

Andy Pearson

CHANGES

To improve is to change; to be perfect is to change often.

Winston Churchill

A dead end is one of the strongest motivations for making people look elsewhere. It is the good people that leave a sinking ship, and the dead wood that stays.

Michael Stern

CHARACTER
See also Being Yourself; Depending on Yourself.

Character equals destiny.

Heraclitus

Faced with a difficult situation, it's to himself that the man of character turns.

Charles de Gaulle

CHARITY
See also Philanthropy.

Give regularly the amount that you feel in your heart you should give, and you will find that your revenues will increase more and more.

Napoleon Hill

I still believe in the importance of charity, which means giving to God his just measure of the goods He has seen fit to bestow on you in the form of material gain. When I started out in the franchise business, I didn't know exactly what I was doing by promising God his part if He helped make my enterprise a success: but I now think that that is the reason for my success ever since.

Colonel Sanders

CHILDREN

Here is the bane of existence for rich kids who inherit a fortune from their parents. Their lives are fairy tales, and they're always asking themselves what they would have done without papa. The poor kid complains that he never had a chance, but the rich kid never knows if he accomplished anything on his own. He's never told the truth, just what he wants to hear.

Lee Iacocca

CIRCULATION
See also Money.

Money is always there, but the pockets change.

Gertrude Stein

CIRCUMSTANCE
See also Destiny; Events.

Man is not a creature of circumstances. Circumstances are the creatures of men.

Benjamin Disraeli

Circumstances? I make circumstances!

Napoleon

People are always blaming their circumstances for what they are. I don't believe in circumstances. The people who get on in this world are the people who get up and look for the circumstances they want, and, if they can't find them, make them.

George Bernard Shaw

CLIENTS

There are not a lot of different kinds of client related problems. There is only one problem: some of us don't take good enough care of our clients.

Thomas J. Watson Sr

The customer is always right.

H. Gordon Selfridge

It's not the employer who pays the salaries, it's the client.

Henry Ford

Every client is a king, but a king is only one client among many.

Henry Ford II

No complaints, no explanations.

Henry Ford II

Be everywhere, do everything, and never miss an opportunity to astonish a client.

Margaret Getchell

We always behave as if we were on the point of losing all our clients.

Jacques Maisonrouge

CLOTHES
See also Appearances.

Clothes don't make the man, but they help a lot as far as businessmen are concerned.

Thomas J. Watson Sr

COLLABORATION
See also Co-operation; Management; Motivation

You scratch my back and I'll scratch yours.

Artemus Ward

In Japan, a company doesn't start out with an entrepreneur who wants his workers to play the role of tools. He creates his company and hires personnel to help him carry out his ideas. Once hired, the personnel are considered collaborators and not machines to make money.

Akio Morita

If I'd had to manage my company myself, I would have very quickly gone bankrupt.

Soichiro Honda

COMMERCE

No nation was ever ruined by commerce.

Benjamin Franklin

COMMITTEES

The number one book of the ages was written by a committee, and it was called *The Bible*.

Louis B. Mayer

A committee is a gathering of important people who singly can do nothing, but together can decide that nothing can be done.

Fred Allen

Here are the rules I have formulated, based on the numerous committees I have sat on. Never arrive on time — if you do, people will think you're a beginner. Don't say anything until half way through the meeting — people will think you're wise. Be as vague as possible — this will help you avoid irritating others. When in doubt, suggest forming a sub-committee. Always be the first to call for an adjournment — this will make you popular, since that's what everyone's waiting for anyway.

Henry Chapman

A committee: a group of people who keep minutes and waste hours.

Milton Berle

Nothing is ever accomplished by a committee, unless it's made up of three persons, one of whom is sick and another absent.

Henrik Van Loon

Nothing stands still down here. I like duck hunting because you have to be fast. You can aim at the duck, have it in your sights — it won't change the direction it's flying in. If you want to hit it, you have to move your rifle. A committee, faced with an important decision, cannot always act quickly enough. When it's finally ready to give its approval, the duck is out of range.

Lee Iacocca

COMMON SENSE

Buy low, sell high, deposit quickly and pay late.

Dick Levin

It is better to have a permanent income than to be fascinating.

Oscar Wilde

I want a good soup, and not beautiful language.

Molière

COMPANIES

To open a company is very easy; to keep it open is very difficult.

Chinese proverb

A company that makes nothing but money is a poor kind of business.

Henry Ford

Go and work in a large company; it's like getting on a train. You're always asking yourself if it is you or the train that's moving at a hundred miles an hour.

John Paul Getty

Creating a company is an experience full of terror and trouble.

Allen Michels

One of the advantages of being new in a company is that you are completely unaware of what is impossible to do.

Peter Peterson

COMPENSATION

The admonition to render more service and better service than that for which one is paid is paradoxical, because it is impossible for anyone to render such service without receiving appropriate compensation. The compensation may come in many forms and from many different sources, some of them strange and unexpected sources, but it will.

Napoleon Hill

If you serve an ungrateful master, serve him the more. Put God in your debt. Every stroke shall be repaid. The longer the payment is with-holden, the better it is for you; compound interest on compound interest is the rate and usage of this exchequer.

Ralph Waldo Emerson

COMPETITION

The art of war is to defeat the enemy without fighting.

Sun Tzu

Competition brings out the best in products, and the worst in people.

David Sarnoff

I have a taste for competition — to always do better, more, always more.

Bernard Tapie

Once in the game, I always try to hit the ball back, and do my best to beat the opponent!

John Paul Getty

In business, the competition bites you if you run, and devours you if you stand still.

William Knudson

The business world has its own corrective mechanism: a director's mistakes become the competition's assets.

Leo Cherne

Forget your opponents: play against your handicap.

Sam Snead

Too many people fear competition, and repudiate success because they're not willing to make the effort or personal sacrifice. That's the problem with society today.

Knute Rockne

The rise and reknown of the Japanese in today's business world, the life blood of our industrial machine, is just good old competition. It is very severe competition, so severe that I'm afraid it might spread to other countries.

Akio Morita

There is always room at the top.

Daniel Webster

COMPLEXES

Take care of your body. Be as good to it as possible. Don't worry about incidents. Look at me — there's nothing of the Greek God about my physique. But I didn't waste any time crying about the unpleasant aspects of my person. And remember that things are only as ugly as you believe they are.

Aristotle Onassis

I imagined him to have a physique as imposing and strong as his reputation merited. When I discovered from reading history books that he was a small man, I was not at all disillusioned. I'm not very big myself, and it was obvious that you don't measure a man's greatness by his physical size, but by his acts, by the impact he makes on human history. I also learned that Napoleon was of humble origin, that probably his family was very poor. So it wasn't necessary to be born a nobleman or rich to succeed in life. There are other qualities which also lead to success. Courage, perseverance, the ability to dream and to persevere.

Soichiro Honda

COMPREHENSION

How many times it thundered before Franklin took the hint. How many apples fell on Newton's head before he took the hint. Nature is always hinting at us. It hints over and over again. And suddenly we take the hint.

Robert Frost

COMPUTERS

A computer cannot replace judgement, just like a pen

cannot replace literary talent. But have you ever tried to write without a pen?

Robert McNamara

All the computers, reports, surveys, and staff analyses provided us with only one thing: information — factual information and sometimes misinformation. When it came time to make a decision, I would ask one, two, or several people, 'What do you think?' From the interchange of ideas, one sparking the other, based upon the facts at hand, we would reach a decision, for better or worse.

Harold Geneen

A computer will not make a good manager out of a bad manager. It makes a good manager better faster and a bad manager worse faster.

Edward M. Esber

Man is still the most extraordinary computer of all.

John F. Kennedy

CONCENTRATION

Don't disperse your forces. Once occupied with a thing, stick to it until you succeed, or until there is absolutely no hope. By pounding a nail with a hammer, you end up by getting it in, if it can go in. When a man's attention is totally concentrated on a single object, he will find better ways, better procedures which he wouldn't have discovered if he'd been thinking about a dozen different projects, splitting his brain and all his senses. More than once, a fortune has slipped through someone's hands because he undertook too much at the same time. 'Don't hunt two hares simultaneously' says the proverb, and the proverb is right.

P.T. Barnum

I got myself completely absorbed in my job as apprentice inventor. I let no one disturb my concentration, not even my friends with whom I enjoyed spending time and doing a thousand things. 'Time for supper!' My mother had to force me to come to the table, since my mind was elsewhere, my ears blocked. 'I'm coming!' I would answer politely, and then get back to work. So she ended up by respecting my work and letting me finish what I had to do. Even hunger could not disturb me.

Soichiro Honda

The ordinary man is rarely in control of his actions: rather it's the actions that control him. Actions should resemble those of a knight, who transforms what to others is an ordinary habit, in other words an unconscious action, into a sacred ritual. This means being aware of what you're doing, concentrated on the present moment.

Tasle d'Heliand

I've always believed that if you stick to a thought and carefully avoid distraction along the way, you can fulfill a dream. My whole life has been about fulfilling dreams. I kept my eye on the target, whatever that target was. Whether your target is big or small, grand or simple, ambitious or personal, I've always believed that success comes from not letting your eyes stray from that target. Anyone who wants to achieve a dream must stay strong, focused and steady.

Estée Lauder

CONCISENESS

Would you be so good as to specify for me, right now, on one single sheet of paper, in what condition the Royal Navy is to face the demands of modern warfare.

Winston Churchill

CONFIDENCE

Self-trust is the first secret of success.

Ralph Waldo Emerson

Physical activity is part of my lifestyle. All managers should know to what extent physical exercise, practiced hard, is good not only for the heart, but also for the mind; it gives you a calm sense of confidence in yourself. And having self-confidence is very important.

Akio Morita

CONTENTMENT
See also Happiness.

Our contentment doesn't depend on what we do, or on where we find ourselves; it depends on what we think.

Dale Carnegie

A person who is not content with others is never content with himself.

Alain

You should always tell yourself, 'It's not at all because of my success that I'm content, it's because I was content that I succeed.'

Alain

CONTRACTS

A verbal contract isn't worth the paper it's written on.

Samuel Goldwyn

CONTROL

A President is either constantly on top of events or, if he hesitates, events will soon be on top of him. I never felt that I could let up for a single moment.

Harry S. Truman

CONVICTION
See also Convincing.

I believed we had created a marvellous appliance, and I was full of hope. But our marketing team was not enthusiastic. I heard that the device was unsellable, and I felt a little embarrassed at having been so passionate about something that others considered a dud. But I had so much confidence in the success of this device, that I claimed personal responsibility for the project. And I never had reason to regret my decision. The idea was approved, and right from the start the Walkman was a smashing success.

Akio Morita

CONVINCING

By battling and arguing, you might succeed in confounding your listener, but your victory will be in vain, because you will never obtain the sincere agreement of your adversary.

Franklin Roosevelt

CO-OPERATION
See also Collaboration; Management; Motivation

When a group of individual brains are co-ordinated and function in harmony, the increased energy created through that alliance becomes available to every individual brain in the group.

Napoleon Hill

People can accomplish things together that they cannot do on their own. By uniting their energies and minds, they create an almost omnipotent force.

Daniel Webster

The best way to exploit ideas is to act as a group with your colleagues. That is why I plan frequent meetings which are sometimes informal among management.

Lee Iacocca

CORPORATE IDENTITY

I was of the conviction that a company's logo was its vital breath, and that it should be defended tenaciously. The logo and name of a company are not just a simple play on words; they evoke the quality of its products and are their guarantee.

Akio Morita

COST

I ascribe the success of the Standard Oil Company to the consistent policy of making its business large through the merit and cheapness of its products.

John Rockefeller

COURAGE
See also Cowardice.

It is more often in the little things than in big ones that we discover courageous people.

Baldassare Castiglione

COWARDICE
See also Courage.

The majority of people are ready to throw their aims and purposes overboard, and give up at the first sign of opposition or misfortune.

Napoleon Hill

CREATIVITY
See also Innovation.

We have always encouraged our employees to have original thoughts, and they have always come through for us. From the entrepreneur's point of view, it's important to know how to liberate the creativity innate in everyone. My opinion is that we all possess creativity, but very few know how to use it. For me there's a solution: always set yourself a goal.

Akio Morita

CREDIT
See also Banks, Borrowing; Buying.

In God we trust . . .everyone else pays cash.

Posted in stores during the Great Depression

It's better to give than to lend, and it doesn't cost any more.

Sir Phillip Gibbs

CREDO

I believe in God, and I believe that through prayer you can attain love of God. I believe in my country. I believe its destiny is noble and great. I believe in truth. I believe that a man who voluntarily lies is a man who voluntarily mutilates himself. But I especially believe in courage, and in enthusiasm, because without these the individual crushes his deepest desires.

Conrad Hilton

You cannot bring about prosperity by discouraging thrift. You cannot help the wage-earner by pulling down the wage-payer. You cannot further the Brotherhood of Man by encouraging class hatred. You cannot help the poor by destroying the rich. You cannot keep out of trouble by spending more than you earn. You cannot build character and courage by taking away a man's initiative. You cannot help men permanently by doing for them what they could and should do for themselves.

Abraham Lincoln

CRISIS
See also Adversity; Defeat; Failure; Struggle.

There's a recession when your neighbour loses his job: there's a crisis when you lose yours.

Harry S. Truman

It seems that the only thing you can count on in the United States is that even during the strongest recessions, the rich keep getting richer.

Lee Iacocca

CRITICISM
See also Critics.

Sandwich every bit of criticism between two heavy layers of praise.

Mary Kay Ash

Honest criticism is hard to take, particularly from a relative, a friend, an acquaintance or a stranger.

Franklin P. Jones

People could disagree with me or with anyone else; they could criticize me or anyone else, and no one would suffer as a consequence. I tried to welcome criticism.

Harold Geneen

For thirty years I've understood that criticism is useless. I have enough trouble correcting my own faults, without tormenting myself because other people aren't perfect.

John Wanamaker

As much as we desire approval, so we dread blame.

Hans Selye

People ask you for criticism, but really all they want is compliments.

W. Somerset Maugham

CRITICS
See also Criticism.

The first idiot to come along is able to criticise, condemn and complain; that's exactly what all idiots do anyway.

Dale Carnegie

Critics are like eunuchs in a harem: they know how it's done, they've seen it done every day, but they're unable to do it themselves.

Brendan Behan

Criticising is easy, and art is difficult.

Philippe Destouche

A business person who goes against the grain of current public opinion has to expect opposition; he or she will be made fun of, and often slandered.

John Paul Getty

Let's say that the person we wish to blame and correct will do everything to justify him or herself, and will blame us in return.

Dale Carnegie

CYNICISM

A cynic is a man who knows the price of all things and the value of none.

Oscar Wilde

D

DEALS

See also Negotiation.

You miss a deal, you get a deal.

American saying

I don't do it for the money. I've got enough, much more than I'll ever need. I do it to do it. Deals are my art form. Other people paint beautifully on canvas or write wonderful poetry. I like making deals, preferably big deals. That's how I get my kicks.

Donald Trump

DEATH

There's no reason to be the richest man in the cemetery. You can't do any business there.

Colonel Sanders

Why retire and wait for death? It will come one day sooner or later anyway, and certainly sooner if you do not do anything.

Rose Blumkin

The moment you stop working, you are dead.

Rita Levi-Montalcini, Nobel Laureate in Physiology

DECISIONS
See also Decisiveness.

From studying hundreds of cases of people who have made large fortunes, it became apparent that these people were in the habit of making very rapid decisions, and of changing their minds with reluctance.

Napoleon Hill

In every success story, you find someone has made a courageous decision.

Peter F. Drucker

A brief written presentation distinguishes the facts from the opinions, and is the basis of all decision making.

Edward G. Harness

Making a decision, even a bad one, is better than making no decision at all.

Jesse Aweida

Every time I make a bad decision, I carry on and make another one.

Harry S. Truman

Bad decisions may be made, but it's the only way to encourage strong people to develop in a company. Crush them and they will suffocate. The best of them will go elsewhere.

Ray Kroc

If I had to sum up what constitutes a good manager in one word, I would say that everything depends on decisions. And a good decision can turn into a bad one if it is applied too late.

Lee Iacocca

From a certain point on, you have to make a decision and press on without looking back.

Wait Phillips

I never varied from the managerial rule that the worst possible thing we could do was to lie dead in the water with any problem. Solve it. Solve it quickly, solve it right or wrong. If you solved it wrong, it would come back and slap you in the face and then you could solve it right. Lying dead in the water and doing nothing is a comfortable alternative because it is without risk, but it is an absolutely fatal way to manage a business.

Thomas J. Watson Sr

I like fast decisions.

Helena Rubinstein

If I had to sum up in one phrase what makes a good manager, I'd say that it's that ability to make decisions.

Lee Iacocca

DECISIVENESS

A man that cannot sit still in his office . . .and that cannot say no . . .is not fit for business.

Samuel Pepys

Any color, as long as it's black [speaking about the Model T Ford].

Henry Ford

DEFEAT
See also Adversity; Crisis; Failure; Struggle.

No one ever is defeated until defeat has been accepted as a reality.

Napoleon Hill

You are not defeated unless you believe you are.

Fernando de Rojas

DELEGATING
See also Employees; Executives.

Nothing is impossible for the man who doesn't have to do it himself.

A.H. Weiler

There are two kinds of work: the first consists of modifying the position of an object in relation to other objects; the second consists in having it done by someone else. The first kind of work is disagreeable and badly paid; the second is pleasant, and well paid.

Bertrand Russell

I always worked on the principle of never having someone else do something that I could do myself. That's how I made my fortune, using the means at my disposal.

Charles de Montesquieu

A good manager surrounds himself with the best people and refrains from interfering in their work.

Theodore Roosevelt

Highly placed individuals who succeed best sort their tasks with the greatest care. They don't try and do everything themselves. They know how to develop and cultivate confidence. In this way they are free to think and plan. They have time to make important calls, and to meet worthwhile people. They also have time to spend with their families.

B.C. Forbes

A first-class man surrounds himself with people who are at least as good, if not better, than himself. A second-class man surrounds himself with third-class people. A third-class man surrounds himself with fifth-class people.

André Weil

When I say to my assistants, 'Never trust anyone', I want them to understand that they shouldn't expect someone else to do a job exactly like they wanted it done, so you shouldn't get someone else to realize your own wishes.

Akio Morita

DELIVERING THE MERCHANDISE

You can't con people, at least not for long. You can create excitement, you can do wonderful promotion and get all kinds of press, and you can throw in a little hyperbole. But if you don't deliver the goods, people will eventually catch on.

Donald Trump

DEPENDING ON YOURSELF
See also Being Yourself; Character.

Your success depends on what you do yourself, with your own means. Don't depend on your friends, and never forget that every man is the sole craftsman of his fortune.

P.T. Barnum

DEPRESSION

When your morale is at its lowest ebb, do something to cheer up someone less fortunate than yourself. You will find arguments to help that person that you haven't thought of for yourself, and which will help you as well.

Sacha Guitry

DESIRE
See also Dreams; Passion.

A man who wants something so much that he is capable of risking his entire future on a simple throw of the dice in order to get it, is sure to succeed.

Napoleon Hill

Anybody can wish for riches, and most people do, but only a few know that a definite plan, plus a burning desire for wealth, are the only dependable means of accumulating wealth.

Napoleon Hill

What you ardently and constantly desire, you always get.

Napoleon

There are two tragedies in life; one is not satisfying your desire, and the other is satisfying it.

Oscar Wilde

DESTINY
See also Circumstance; Events.

A man's destiny is determined by what he thinks of himself.

Henry David Thoreau

Our safety and our peril lie in ourselves.

Epictetus

At certain moments, men are masters of their fate; and if our condition is found wanting, the fault lies not in the stars, but in ourselves.

William Shakespeare

For those who have a mission to accomplish, corporal existence is prolonged as long as is necessary.

The Brahma-Sutra [ancient and sacred Indian text]

What is this thing that Alexander referred to when he spoke about his destiny, that Caesar meant by his luck, Napoleon his star? What is it, if not the confidence each of those three men had that they would play an important role in history.

Charles de Gaulle

Sow a thought and you reap an act;
Sow an act and you reap a habit;
Sow a habit and you reap a character;
Sow a character and you reap a destiny.

Ralph Waldo Emerson

I'm sure you have a theme: the theme of life. You can embellish it or desecrate it, but it's your theme, and as long as you follow it, you will experience harmony and peace of mind.

Agatha Christie

Without destiny, I could have been a *maître d'*.

Charlie Chaplin

Destiny, the famous 'mektoub' of the Orientals, was above all a superb and terrible mechanism of resignation. I was firmly decided not to fall into the trap of passivity when, observing others clipped and gagged, I suddenly discovered myself. I had caught a glimpse of my limited possibilities, but I was going to work to enlarge my universe to its utmost and started researching its limits, which I knew were greater than I imagined.

Bernard Tapie

The problems we have to face in life . . .I don't believe in destiny, or in pure luck; you have to help it along, just like you have to contribute to the destiny of a business by helping it with reasonable actions. If not, you just keep going round in circles.

Maurice Biderman

Our victory and our loss lie within ourselves.

Epictetus

I most certainly was not born a businessman.

John Paul Getty

Sipping my orange juice, with three cents in my pocket, I wasn't worried; I looked around and listened very calmly, without envy, because I knew that I would soon join the dancers, and that it would be I who would lead the dance.

Régine

DETACHMENT

The true value of a man can be determined by examining to which extent, and in which sense, he is able to liberate himself from his ego.

Albert Einstein

DETAIL

Whoever wants to accomplish great things must devote a lot of profound thought to details.

Paul Valéry

Neglecting small things under the pretext of wanting to accomplish large ones is the excuse of a coward.

Alexandra David-Neel

A handful of men have become very rich simply by paying attention to details that most others ignored.

Henry Ford

I would never have succeeded in life if I hadn't given the same care and attention to the little things as I did to the big.

Charles Dickens

It has long been an axiom of mine that the little things are infinitely the most important.

Sir Arthur Conan Doyle

I was always happy to see my McDonald's again. Sometimes, however, what I saw gave me less pleasure. Sometimes Ed MacLuckie forgot to light up the sign at nightfall, and that made me furious. Or sometimes there was garbage on the grounds, and Ed told me he hadn't had the time to clean it up. These little things didn't seem to disturb him, but for me they were serious. I shouted like a madman, and I was not easy on Ed. He took it all in good humour. I know these details counted as much for him as for me, which he proved in his own restaurants a few years later.

Ray Kroc

Each time I met with failure, I analysed it and always noticed, looking back, that I had ignored an essential aspect of the problem because it had seemed unimportant. It was only later — too late — that I understood its importance. In business, like in love, like in sport, you cannot leave any detail out on the pretext that it's not important.

Bernard Tapie

DETERMINATION
See also Obstacles; Perseverance.

Where the willingness is great, the difficulties cannot be great.

Machiavelli

We will either find a way or make one.

Hannibal

DIFFERENCES

We will have differences. Men of different ancestries, men of different tongues, men of different colors, men of different environments, men of different geographies do not see everything alike. Even in our own country we do not see everything alike. If we did, we would all want the same wife — and that would be a problem, wouldn't it?

Lyndon Baines Johnson

Being a little more than the others each time leads, in the long run, and in the final analysis, to being totally different from others. Each day is a lesson in courage.

Bernard Tapie

Sir, if you and I had the same opinions about the same subjects, it would be useless for both of us to remain with the same company and both receive a salary. If that were the case, one of us should resign. It is precisely because our opinions differ that the company runs less risk of making mistakes.

Akio Morita

DIFFICULTY

Difficulties attract men of character, because in overcoming them he realizes himself.

Charles de Gaulle

Don't tell me this is a difficult problem. If it weren't difficult, it wouldn't be a problem.

Ed Koch

Difficult things can be done right away: impossible things take a little time.

George Santayana

We overcome difficulties simply by lifting our spirits above them. This allows us to conquer all limitations which we impose on ourselves in our mortal consciousness.

Baird T. Spalding

DIPLOMACY
See also Enemies.

A real diplomat is one who can cut his neighbor's throat without having his neighbor notice it.

Trygve Halvdan Lie

DIPLOMAS
See also Education; Master of Business Administration; School.

A diploma is less useful than a ticket to a movie. With the ticket, you can at least enter the movie house and spend an enjoyable evening; but a diploma is by no means a sure ticket to life.

Soichiro Honda

DIRECTION
See also Management.

The key to success depends on people. Direction is nothing else than motivating people.

Lee Iacocca

Respect of the individual is a simple concept, but at IBM directors spend most of their time [in] achieving it.

Thomas J. Watson Sr

DISCIPLINE
See also Self-mastery.

All power comes from discipline and is corrupted as soon as the restraints are neglected.

Roger Caillois

I watched in stupefaction as executives, coffee in hand, strolled aimlessly around the President's office. I understood that anarchy was the order of the day. Chrysler needed a good dose of order and discipline, and quickly.

Lee Iacocca

As a manager, you should impose discipline on yourself. If not, it will be imposed from above.

Robert Wood

You should disobey, but make sure you're right.

Jacky Setton

The discipline you impose on yourself by writing things down is the first step towards getting them done.

Lee Iacocca

DISCOURAGEMENT
See also Advisors; Critics.

All my life people have said I wasn't going to make it.

Ted Turner

DISHONESTY

I admit that I delight in the company of frank and honest men. I have an instinctive horror for dishonesty. I cannot conceive of rejoicing for an instant from having earned a single dollar from cupidity or trickery.

Conrad Hilton

DIVERSITY

In business, as in technology, I adopt the same attitude towards my mistakes or failures: I believe they are inevitable, but useful. Moving forward necessitates risk. The important thing is to be able to adapt and be sufficiently diversified so that a single mistake doesn't compromise your entire future.

An Wang

The only salvation . . .is for a company to produce several different products, so that when the demand for one goes down, the company can deploy its assets to the products for which there is a demand.

Harold Geneen

DOUBT
See also Confidence; Hesitation.

Anything you become involved with must be worth your total commitment. Do you believe it has a chance to make it? Going into a venture with large doubts is writing a script for its failure. When the terrain gets rocky — and every entrepreneurial venture has its share of hard times — it's not likely that you will give the project the support it requires if you don't trust in its merits.

Victor Kiam

For me, doubt carries feelings of guilt along with it, which in turn engender resignation and discouragement. I was very moved by something I read in Gramsci about doubt: 'The pessimism of intelligence, the optimism of action.' That could be my motto.

Bernard Tapie

DREAMS
See also Desire.

I have never been stingy with my dreams.

Paul Ricard

My formula: dream, risk and humour.

Bernard Tapie

The moment had come to start working on realizing another dream. Trying to win Formula 1 was for many trying to accomplish the impossible. But my decision was made, once and for all. I would have to put in the necessary time, but nothing could stop me from succeeding.

Soichiro Honda

If you can dream it, you can do it.

Walt Disney

All men dream, but not equally. Those who dream by night in the dusty recesses of their minds wake in the day to find that it was vanity. But the dreamers of the day are the dangerous men, for they may act on their dream with open eyes, to make it possible.

T.E. Lawrence

What you call dreams are real for the fighters.

Bernard Tapie

The point is that you can dream great dreams, but they'll never amount to much if you can't turn them into reality at a reasonable cost.

Donald Trump

First comes the shy wish. Then you must have the heart to have the dream. Then, you work. And work.

Estée Lauder

Dreams, risks and laughter — three words which I have always used to direct my life.

Bernard Tapie

DUTY

I believe the power to make money is a gift of God . . .to be developed and used to the best of our ability for the good of mankind. Having been endowed with the gift I possess,

I believe it is my duty to make money, and still more money, and to use the money I make for the good of my fellow man according to the dictates of my conscience.

John Rockefeller

E

EASE

You usually discover that if you make things easier for people, you gain their sympathy.

Aristotle Onassis

ECONOMISTS

An economist is someone who explains the evidence in obscure terms.

Alfred Knopf

If all the economists were laid end to end, they still wouldn't reach a conclusion.

George Bernard Shaw

If economists were good in business, they would be rich men, instead of experts advising rich men.

Kirk Kerkorian

EDUCATION
See also Diplomas; School.

When I was not busy cutting wood, I worked on combustion engines, studying their character and the way they worked. I read everything I could find on the subject, but it's from my own practice that I got the best education.

Henry Ford

Everyone gets two kinds of education: one which is provided by others, and another, much more important, which comes from yourself.

Edward Gibbon

When I started in 1951, I don't think anyone could have predicted that I'd become the boss of a company worth three billion dollars. But I did learn what was needed to get there. I am convinced that you don't have to study to direct a business. On the other hand, you do need great powers of observation, you have to know how to try out theories, and gain knowledge from your errors. There are a host of people like us. If you look at who the directors are of the 1000 club, you'll find that a good many of them never had a higher education, and are ex-mechanics, salesmen or office clerks.

An Wang

Let me remind you that I have a row of electric buttons in my office. All I have to do is press one of them to call the person who can answer any question on any subject I wish to know, relative to the business at hand. I take care of the business, they take care of the questions. Now would you be so good as to explain why, just to answer your questions, I should have a brain stuffed with general culture, when I am surrounded by employees who can supply any information I might want to know?

Henry Ford

EFFICIENCY

If an employee gets results, I don't care in the least if he shines his shoes with a brick.

John J. Byrne

It doesn't matter if a cat is black or white, so long as it catches mice.

Deng Xiaoping

EFFORT
See also Elbow Grease; Extra Mile; Struggle; Work.

The only place where success comes before work is in the dictionary.

Vidal Sassoon

The life of an entrepreneur is full of sacrifice. Body builders have a saying, 'No pain, no gain.' That should be the credo of every entrepreneur.

Victor Kiam

Try harder every day. There will surely be tomorrows that will bring you a lot of satisfaction and a lot of money.

Thomas J. Watson Sr

I learned fast that you get nothing for nothing.

Régine

EGOTISM

The worst disease which can afflict business executives in their work is not, as popularly supposed, alcoholism; it's egotism.

Harold Geneen

Ego gratification is one of the worst traps devised to ensnare the successful businessman.

Harold Geneen

Empty yourself of you and fill yourself with others.

Abbot Delille

Egotists are people who don't use every minute of their lives to make other egotists happy.

Lucien Guitry

ELBOW GREASE
See also Effort; Extra Mile; Struggle; Work.

Soap, water and elbow grease; those are the three ingredients for success in the hotel business.

Conrad Hilton

ELOQUENCE

The finest eloquence is that which gets things done; the worst is that which delays them.

David Lloyd George

EMPATHY
See also Employees; Human Relations.

A man who can put himself in the place of others, who can understand the mechanism of their thoughts, will never have to worry about what the future holds in store for him.

Owen D. Young

The secret of success — if there is one — is the ability to put yourself in another person's shoes, and to consider things from his or her point of view as well as your own.

Henry Ford

EMPLOYEES
See also Delegation; Empathy; Human Relations; Personnel.

One of the main reasons many people do not advance in their careers is the problems they have working well with their colleagues.

Lee Iacocca

The attention and consideration given even to the lowliest employee has always led to improvement in the business.

Bill Marriott Jr

When a factory gets close to having 1,500 employees, things start derailing.

John Mitchell

Nobody knows more about the obstacles to productivity than the person doing the work.

Thomas Bata

You can confiscate the factories, burn the buildings, but leave me the employees and I'll rebuild my empire.

Thomas J. Watson Sr

Our personnel need a perspective on the future. Without the opportunity for growth, they would all leave.

Donald Burr

The most important thing is the human being. You may have the best projects in the world, or the most sophisticated equipment, but without good employees you have nothing.

Yoshiki Yamasaki

Unusual effort on the part of employees who are apparently ordinary workers is one of the main indications of a superior enterprise.

Thomas Peters and Robert Waterman

You have the employees you deserve.

Sir Walter Bilbey

EMULATION
See also Example.

To get results, stimulate competition, not the sordid competition based on gain alone but rather a more noble emulation; the desire to do better, to surpass others and to surpass oneself.

Charles Schwab

My experience has taught me that the next best thing to being truly great is to emulate the great, in feeling and action, as closely as possible.

Napoleon Hill

ENEMIES
See also Diplomacy.

Forgive your enemies, but never forget their names.

John Fitzgerald Kennedy

Always assume your opponent to be smarter than you.

Walther Rathenau

Don't waste a minute thinking about your enemies.

Dale Carnegie

ENGINEERING

Engineering is the ability to do for one dollar what any damn fool can do for five dollars.

Arthur Mellen Wellington

ENTHUSIASM
See also Ardour; Zeal.

Nothing great was ever achieved without enthusiasm.

Ralph Waldo Emerson

We wanted people who were intelligent, knowledgeable and experienced, but in choosing among candidates who had those attributes, I wanted men around me who shared my enthusiasm for work.

Harold Geneen

It is impossible for a man to live without having some preconceived idea of where his life is going. As far back as I can remember, I was marked with the sign of enthusiasm. With enthusiasm to propel me, and prayer to shield me, I can say that I like what I've done with my life. Inevitably, with such attributes, it is difficult not to lead a full, active, happy life. Give a man the ambition to spur him on, the faith to guide him, and the good health to allow him to fulfil his potential, and he will, in one form or another, achieve success.

Conrad Hilton

Nothing great was ever accomplished without enthusiasm.

Ralph Waldo Emerson

The Greeks gave us the most beautiful word in our language: the word 'enthusiasm' — from the Greek *En Theo* which means 'inner God'.

Louis Pasteur

ENTREPRENEURS

I became a real entrepreneur, crazy enough to take the risk of losing everything.

Ray Kroc

Entrepreneurs are simply those who understand that there is little difference between obstacle and opportunity and are able to turn both to their advantage.

Victor Kiam

I acquired the Remington company in 1979 and put it back on its feet. How I made these acquisitions and revived these companies will be discussed later ... What is important to note here is the fact that I am not a genius. Far from it. I believe that any success I've had can be attributed to my adherence to the entrepreneurial principles I developed early in my career.

Victor Kiam

EQUALITY

Our working relations unfold in an atmosphere of equality which exists nowhere else in the world. At Sony, there is no marked difference between white collar and blue collar workers. Managing is not reigning. Executives of the company must have the necessary qualities to direct the personnel by showing them the way to do things. We are constantly looking for individuals who possess these qualities. Putting people down, because they lack diplomas or because they're having trouble with a certain job, is a sign of incompetence. There is very little rivalry in our company. Succeeding by creating conflict is impossible.

Akio Morita

If all the money and property in the world were divided up equally at, say, 3 o'clock in the afternoon, by 3.30 p.m. there would already be notable differences in the financial conditions of the recipients. Within that first 30 minutes, some adults would have lost their share. Some would have gambled theirs away and some would have been swindled or cheated out of their portion (thereby making some others richer). The disparity would increase with growing momentum as time went on. After 90 days, the differences would be staggering. And, I'm willing to wager that, within a year or two at the most, the distribution of wealth would conform to patterns almost identical with those that had previously prevailed.

John Paul Getty

EQUANIMITY

It's your money that is invested in the venture or, at the very least, your drive and energy that is keeping a project afloat. Everybody working for and with you will take their cue from you. If you're down, the company is down. You must maintain equanimity. I'm lucky; I can share my troubles with my young lady, my wife, Ellen. But in the presence of my employees, all fear or sense of desperation must be suppressed. I've made it a practice not to let people know whether I'm up or down; I try to keep the same face in all circumstances.

Victor Kiam

ERRORS
See also Perfection.

What is the secret of the Apple Corporation? Well, we hire very qualified people and then we create an environment where they can commit errors and develop themselves.

Steven Jobs

If I haven't committed any errors, it is because I haven't made any decisions.

General Johnson

If you close the door to all error, then the truth will stay outside.

Rabindranâth Tagore

And those who do nothing are never wrong.

Théodore de Banville

It is possible that all the mistakes lead to an inestimable gain.

Goethe

We have the perfect right to make mistakes, as long as we are doing what we like. On the other hand, it is unpardonable to have done what we do not like, especially if we are a success.

Christian Dior

Move forward and do what you think is best. If you make a mistake, you'll learn something. But don't make the same mistake twice.

Akio Morita

The greatest right in the world is the right to be wrong.

William Randolph Hearst

A life full of error is not only more honorable, but more useful than a life dedicated to doing nothing.

George Bernard Shaw

The greatest error a man can make is to be afraid to make one.

Elbert Hubbard

The greatest general is he who makes the fewest mistakes.

Napoleon

Everybody makes mistakes. Ibuka and I made quite a few. We lost money on the Chromaton process, and we failed with the L-cassette (a large format audio cassette which would have created better sound than the quarter inch cassettes currently on the market). We also had to unite a number of companies to keep the Beta-max format alive. But the important thing is that these errors are human and natural; in the long run, they did not compromise the future of the company.

Akio Morita

EVENTS
See also Circumstance; Destiny

When I cannot direct events any longer, I let them direct themselves.

Henry Ford

EXAMPLE
See also Direction; Emulation; Management.

Example is leadership.

Albert Schweitzer

EXCELLENCE
See also Perfection.

Spend whatever it takes to build the best. Then let people

know about it. In New York, there is no limit to how much money people will spend for the very best, not second best, the very best.

Donald Trump

It is better to aim for perfection and miss the target than to aim for imperfection and achieve it.

Thomas J. Watson Sr

The company that ignores excellence in its plumbing, and that tolerates inaccuracies in its philosophy, will have neither good plumbing nor good philosophy. Neither the pipes nor the theories will hold.

John Gardner

Whatever is worth doing at all, is worth doing well.

Philip Dormer Stanhope

If a man can write a better book, preach a better sermon, or make a better mouse-trap than his neighbor, though he builds his house in the woods, the world will make a beaten path to his door.

Ralph Waldo Emerson

Few people dare get into business because, deep down, they say to themselves: 'Why should I put such and such a product on the market when somebody else is producing it already?' As for me, I've always said: 'Why not do better?' And that's what I did.

Henry Ford

EXCELLING

Men of genius do not excel in any profession because they labour in it, but they labour in it because they excel.

William Hazlitt

EXCUSES

The buck stops here.

Harry S. Truman

If you want to do something, you find a way. If you don't want to do anything, you find an excuse.

Arab proverb

EXECUTIVES
See also Delegating

I firmly believe in the Peter Principle, which states that executives have a tendency to reach their highest level of incompetence.

William G. McGowan

There's more merit and satisfaction in being a first-rate truck driver than a tenth-rate executive.

B.C. Forbes

The success of my business is due in large part to my insight in choosing the persons to occupy key positions.

Ray Kroc

Any executive worth the title prefers dealing with people who aim too high than with those who are timid.

Lee Iacocca

Personal productivity of high-ranking executives is a vital ingredient for a company's success.

Rene McPherson

Average executives are like sponges. In most businesses they play only a minor role on the working team, consisting mainly of latching on to ideas as they filter up from below, and vice versa.

Ed Carlson

I think if you have two executives who think alike, then one of them is superfluous.

Ray Kroc

EXERCISE

When the body is weak, it commands. When it's strong, it obeys.

Jean-Jacques Rousseau

I belong to the group of people who like their work, but who also like to play. I started tennis at 55, ski-ing at 60, and I started water ski-ing again at 64, but it hurts too much in the legs. I've been playing golf for 40 years, and I still love the game with my 16 handicap. Every Tuesday morning we have a director's meeting in Tokyo, and when I'm in Japan I always try to attend. But I always go to the indoor tennis court first, next door to the office, and at 7 and 9 o'clock I play a few sets.

Akio Morita

Do enough exercise and keep yourself in shape. Practicing basic yoga is recommended, both for the body and the mind. If you can do Judo for an hour or two a week, you can get rid of all your complexes.

Aristotle Onassis

EXPANSION

The golden rule of success is expansion!

John Rockefeller

EXPECTATION

My experience with people is that they generally do what you expect them to do! If you expect them to perform well, they will; conversely, if you expect them to perform poorly, they'll probably oblige.

Mary Kay Ash

EXPERIENCE

Many men who supposedly have ten years' experience really only have one year's experience repeated ten times.

Roger Falk

In the business world, everyone is paid in two kinds of coin: cash and experience. Take the experience first, the cash will come later.

Harold Geneen

If you think of a giant human memory bank in operation, each of those General Managers Meetings had an average of 120 highly competent men, each with more than 20 years of business experience from all parts of the world and with different product lines. That's 2,400 years of business managerial experience on hand for each of our meetings. And we had two of them, every month.

Harold Geneen

Life is work, and everything you retain adds to your experience.

Henry Ford

Experience is the most efficient tool for transforming innovation into action.

Peter Peterson

No success without a sure sense of judgement. Judgement is formed by experience. You acquire experience by making errors in judgement.

Arthur Jones

Experience does not err; only your judgements err by expecting from her what is not in her power.

Leonardo da Vinci

I don't want men of experience working for me. The experienced man is always telling me why something can't be done. He is smart; he is intelligent; he thinks he knows the answers. The fellow who has not had any experience is so dumb he doesn't know a thing can't be done — and he goes ahead and does it.

Charles F. Kettering

Does he have 17 years of experience or one year of experience 17 times?

Paul R. Wiesenfeld

'Well, you'll never have enough experience until one day, young fellow, you'll have enough experience.' And he paused, looked me in the eye and added, 'But then you'll be too old.'

Harold Geneen

Experience is a name men give to their mistakes.

Oscar Wilde

When a person with experience meets a person with money, pretty soon, the person with the experience will have the money and the person with the money will have the experience.

Estée Lauder

EXPERTS

All you have to do is to be correct in your predictions three times in a row, and then you can call yourself an expert.

Laurence Peter

An expert is one who knows more and more about less and less.

Nicholas Murray Butler

EXTRA MILE
See also Effort; Elbow Grease; Struggle; Work.

If a man performs no more service than that for which he is being paid, then obviously he is receiving all the pay to which he is entitled.

Napoleon Hill

Give more service and better service than you are paid for. Find out more about your job, and the job above yours, than you absolutely have to know. Work in a way that makes your job do more than it is expected to do for the organization that employs you.

Napoleon Hill

I never limited myself to serving gas. I also repaired flat tires that customers left at the station. The service station was open until 9 o'clock, then when I closed I repaired the inner tubes. Sometimes I didn't finish working until 1 or 2 o'clock in the morning. Then I opened again at 5 a.m. Most gas stations didn't open until 7, and I sold more gas between 5 and 7 in the morning than the other stations sold all day.

Colonel Sanders

At 5 o'clock, the day people and the demands they make on you are gone. You can sit at your desk, alone, and realize that now you can do exactly what you want to do. The buzzer on your desk will summon one of your two secretaries. Your limousine and chauffeur await below. Your plane is at a nearby airport. You can go anywhere you want. Perhaps you have a computer terminal on your desk. You can check out the winning scores on the stock market for that day, or you can check the theatre shows in London or New York. There is almost always a dinner invitation you could accept. But there is also that 'homework' on your desk, waiting.

Harold Geneen

Courage lies in accepting that you have to go farther when you feel your mind and body have reached their limit.

Bernard Tapie

F

FACTS
See also Detail; Knowledge; Wisdom

The highest art of professional management requires the ability to literally 'smell' a real fact from all others — and moreover to have the temerity, intellectual curiosity, guts and/or plain impoliteness, if necessary, to be sure what you have is indeed what we call an 'unshakable fact'.

Harold Geneen

FAILURE
See also Adversity; Crisis; Defeat; Struggle.

No one succeeds in all they try to do, and our existence always includes some measure of failure. The important thing is not to weaken at the moment of truth, and maintain our efforts right up to the end of our lives.

Joseph Conrad

I think that each of the failures I had to face provided me with the opportunity of starting again and trying something new.

Colonel Sanders

Failures are like skinned knees ...painful but superficial, they heal quickly.

H. Ross Perot

Successful entrepreneurs average about 3.8 failures before achieving final success.

Lisa M. Amoss

The first law of holes: When you're in a hole, you have to stop digging.

Benjamin Franklin

You mustn't refuse to admit to failure because of pride. Just make a mark and get on to something else. A good thing about life is that people mostly remember success. Failures are quickly forgotten.

Daniel Filipacchi

Transform failure into success!

John Rockefeller

Failure — especially if experienced early enough — serves to build the warrior. Rumours of the setbacks that anyone who takes risks is sure to encounter can too quickly weigh heavily on the shoulders of an entrepreneur ... I reserve the right to fail as fundamental; it allows for clear-headed people, with resilient souls to rebound and go farther than they ordinarily would.

Bernard Tapie

Sometimes by losing a battle you find a new way to win the war. What you need, generally, is enough time and a little luck.

Donald Trump

A hatred of failure has always been part of my nature and, I suppose, one of the more pronounced motivating forces in my life. It is not that I love success for its own sake. However, once I have committed myself to any undertaking, a powerful inner drive cuts in and I become intent on seeing it through to a satisfactory conclusion. In most fields of endeavour, I have been successful more often than not. When my efforts resulted in failure, I did everything possible to ensure that my mistakes were not repeated.

John Paul Getty

Double your rate of failure . . . Failure is a teacher — a harsh one, perhaps, but the best . . . That's what I have to do when an idea back-fires or a sales program fails. You've got to put failure to work for you . . . You can be discouraged by failure or you can learn from it. So go ahead and make mistakes. Make all you can. Because that's where you will find success. On the far side of failure.

Thomas J. Watson Sr

FAITH
See also Confidence; Hope

Your subconscious starts to function according to the universal law: Whatever the mind can conceive of and believe in, it can obtain.

Napoleon Hill

Everything is possible. Faith is the substance of our hopes, the guarantor of what we've never seen.

Henry Ford

Profound belief in something allows every individual to find an immense inner force, and to overcome his or her failings.

Soichiro Honda

When Jesus said, 'I am the doorway', he meant that in every soul 'I am' is the doorway through which God expresses His life, His power and His being through the individual. 'I am' is expressed in different ways on four levels: concept, thought, word, and action. This power, this substance, this intelligence of the eternal is modelled by the conscience. That's why the Master said: 'Act according to your faith.' And also: 'Everything is possible to the person who believes.'

Baird T. Spalding

When you really believe in what you're doing, you must persevere despite all obstacles.

Lee Iacocca

FAMILY
See also Friends

The navigator who knows that a line connects his raft to the dock will be less afraid than the one who floats helplessly on the currents. Those who worry about the future and splash about anxiously have lost their point of reference: notably the family, friends, and solidarity with their peers.

Bernard Tapie

FEAR
See also Courage

A man without fear succeeds in everything he undertakes.

Napoleon Hill

The only thing we have to fear is fear itself.

Franklin Roosevelt

Never negotiate in fear; but don't be afraid to negotiate.

John Fitzgerald Kennedy

FINANCE
See also Capital; Circulation; Money

Finance is the art of passing currency from hand to hand until it finally disappears.

Robert W. Sarnoff

Champions of finance are like pearls in a necklace: when one falls, all the others follow.

Henrik Ibsen

FIRSTS
See also Ambition; Motivation

I prefer being the first man here than the second in Rome.

Julius Caesar

I wanted to be first, so I forged myself the destiny of a star or a queen.

Régine

It's always better to be first in a small company than second in a large one.

Marcel Dassault

FLEXIBILITY

I protect myself by being flexible. I never get too attached to one deal or one approach. For starters, I keep a lot of balls in the air, because most deals fall out, no matter how promising they seem at first. In addition, once I've made a deal, I always come up with at least a half dozen approaches to making it work, because anything can happen, even to the best-laid plans.

Donald Trump

Convince me that I'm wrong and I'll quickly apologize and change my ways.

Robert Maxwell

FOLLY
See also Errors

I resolved to proceed on a large scale of massive, high-priced purchases, and to build an independent petroleum enterprise. My friends and acquaintances — to say nothing of my competitors — thought that my buying binge constituted a fatal error.

John Paul Getty

It has always been apparent that in order to succeed in the world, you have to seem crazy and be wise.

Charles de Montesquieu

Howard Hughes was able to afford the luxury of madness, like a man who not only thinks he is Napoleon, but hires an army to prove it.

Ted Morgan

It is not wise to compliment a person on his success, because too often actions which were undertaken with the best logic come to an unhappy conclusion, while mad projects succeed.

Sir Walter Raleigh

FORESIGHT
See also Anticipation

In business, like in the martial arts, the essential thing is not just to deflect blows, but to foresee where they're coming from.

Bernard Tapie

It's been said that I believe in the power of positive thinking. In fact, I believe in the power of negative thinking. I happen to be very conservative in business. I always go into the deal anticipating the worst. If you plan for the worst — if you can live with the worst — the good will always take care of itself.

Donald Trump

FORGETTING

Forgetting is the great secret of strong and creative lives.

Honoré de Balzac

FREEDOM

Every slave has it in his power to break the bonds of his servitude.

William Shakespeare

People are prisoners of everything they do not own.

Anwar Sadat

Remember that thoughts and spoken words are things. Proclaim the news of your joy and be free, completely free of all limitation. Then know that you are free, and triumphantly pursue your chosen path in total freedom.

Baird T. Spalding

For me, money has never had the sound of anything else but freedom.

Coco Chanel

No man is free who is not master of himself.

Epictetus

Drive thy business; let it not drive thee.

Benjamin Franklin

I finally became an independent man, a real man, master of his arms, legs, head, destiny, of his timetable and the risks he knew he should take.

Soichiro Honda

FREE ENTERPRISE

The business of government is to keep government out of business, unless business needs its help.

Will Rogers

Agriculture, industry, commerce and navigation — the four pillars of economy — prosper most when they are left in the hands of free enterprise.

Thomas Jefferson

FRIENDS
See also Enemies; Family

No one is completely unhappy at the failure of his best friend.

Groucho Marx

The richer your friends, the more they cost you.

Elisabeth Marbury

Money doesn't make as many true friends as real enemies.

Thomas Fuller

You have to be ready to carry your cross if you want to become the head of a large business: you'll lose many of your friends on the way.

Ray Kroc

Better have rich friends who can help you than poor friends whom you can't always help.

Marcel Dassault

Rich people are usually suspicious. They're afraid that everyone either wants their time, their money or their reputation.

Francoise Sagan

My father always said that if you have five true friends when you die, your life has been a success.

Lee Iacocca

The friendship of a great man is a gift of the gods.

Voltaire

The difficult thing is not to stand by your friends when they're right, but when they're wrong.

André Malraux

A friendship born of business is better than a business born of friendship.

John Rockefeller

A lot of my friends told me I'd be better off staying in my garage, growing little by little, letting my business prosper in this way rather than undertaking risky adventures. I had invested all my savings in this operation. I felt responsible to those with whom I'd gotten involved, and I said to myself that by closing my garage at the age of 30, I had perhaps missed my chance and sunk my own ship.

Soichiro Honda

Wait for the night to come, and don't celebrate until your thinking is done. Then enjoy a good meal in the company of friends, and try to avoid talking about business at the table.

Aristotle Onassis

FRUSTRATION

There's nothing more frustrating than seeing something that doesn't work and having to explain it to a hard-headed boss who you know won't listen anyway: Everyone knows that, since antiquity, petty rulers hate bearers of bad tidings, or those whose thinking goes against the grain. After some time, I decided that the best way to prove my predictions correct was to carry them out on my own, as I wished.

Bernard Tapie

FUN

I don't kid myself. Life is very fragile, and success doesn't change that. If anything, success makes it more fragile. Anything can change, without warning, and that's why I try not to take any of what's happened too seriously. Money was never a big motivation for me, except as way to keep score. The real excitement is playing the game. I don't spend a lot of time worrying about what I should have done differently, or what's going to happen next. If you ask me exactly what the deals I'm about to describe all add up to in the end, I'm not sure I have a very good answer. Except that I've had a very good time making them.

Donald Trump

It never stops, and I wouldn't have it any other way. I try to learn from the past, but I plan for the future by focusing exclusively on the present. That's where the fun is. And if it can't be fun, what's the point?

Donald Trump

FURNITURE

Upgrading office furniture is not very important to Japanese management. Striving to obtain an office with a couch, a water fountain and an original work of art on the wall does not interest our executives.

Akio Morita

G

GAMES

After a certain point, money is meaningless. It ceases to be the goal. The game is what counts.

Aristotle Onassis

GENERAL COSTS

Everyone knows that organized crime in the United States generates more than 40 billion dollars in yearly revenues. The benefits are considerable, especially if you account for the minimal expenses the Mafia has to cover for office furniture!

Woody Allen

GENEROSITY

I wanted to help people. At the time of the W.P.A. (Work Project Administration) I aided a number of families, even though I was poor myself. I have always given money to the church, and supported religious works.

Colonel Sanders

You always have to replenish the well where you get your water. If not, it'll dry up!

Steven Spielberg

GENIUS
See also Talent

Genius is one percent inspiration and ninety-nine percent perspiration.

Thomas Alva Edison

The man of genius is someone who gives me some.

Paul Valéry

Ah! Beat on your heart, that's where genius lies.

Alfred de Musset

There is no genius without a seed of madness.

Aristotle

Let us say that men of genius are those who can do quickly what we do slowly.

Joseph Joubert

When a true genius appears in the world, you may know him by this sign: That all the dunces are in confederacy against him.

Jonathan Swift

There are geniuses in trade as well as in war, or the state, or letters; and the reason why this or that man is fortunate is not to be told. It lies in the man: that is all anybody can tell you about it.

Ralph Waldo Emerson

The difference between genius and stupidity is that genius has its limits.

Anonymous

Genius is quite simply the ability to reduce that which is complicated to something simple.

C.W. Ceram

I have nothing to declare except my genius.

Oscar Wilde

Genius is only a greater aptitude for patience.

Buffon

GETTING AHEAD
See also Success

Our business is not to get ahead of others, but to get ahead of ourselves.

Thomas L. Monson

GIVING

When we began our adoptee programme, it was generally felt that it wouldn't work. But I knew it would. I knew it would work because it was based on the Golden Rule. At Mary Kay Cosmetics we sometimes call it the 'go-give' principle. It's a philosophy based on giving, and it is applied in every aspect of our business. At our beauty shows we do not like a beauty consultant to think, 'How much can I sell these women?' Instead we stress, 'What can I do to make these women leave here today feeling better about themselves? How can I help them have a better self-image?'

Mary Kay Ash

Loving is opening the limitless reservoir of the golden treasure of God. Whoever loves cannot prevent himself from giving. And giving is gaining. So goes the law of love. By giving, we put the infallible law of 'measure for measure' in motion. By giving with no ulterior motive of receiving in return, you cannot help but receive, because what you gave will come back to you according to the law. 'Give and you shall receive, in full measure shall your cup overflow.' This is how you are nourished. Because you will be measured by the same measure that you have used to measure what you give.

Baird T. Spalding

Whatever you give comes back to you.

Estée Lauder

GLORY

He who really wants glory ends up by getting it, or at least coming very close. But you have to want it, and not only once. You have to want it each moment.

Marie-Jean Hérault de Sechelles

Glory is given only to those who have always dreamed of it.

Charles de Gaulle

GOALS

A three-sentence course on business management: You read a book from the beginning to the end. You run a business the opposite way. You start with the end, and then you do everything you must to reach it. The beauty of setting a realistic, firm objective — or as I said, starting out with the end — is that the goal itself will begin to define what it is you have to do to attain it.

Harold Geneen

Better get a stiff neck from aiming too high than a hunch back from aiming too low.

Jacques Chancel

All of a sudden I realized that I'd covered a lot of ground towards achieving the goal I had set myself, and which I had undertaken in September of 1914. I had established the base for my own business in the American petroleum industry. I wasn't quite 24 years old, but I had become a successful independent petroleum dealer. And I'd made my first million.

John Paul Getty

Three to five goals per year is the maximum.

John Hanley

In enterprises that succeed, there is a consensus of the entire hierarchy on the collection of global goals.

John Young

Management through goals works if you know your objectives. But ninety per cent of the time, this is not the case.

Peter F. Drucker

To become a billionaire, you have to have the mentality of a billionaire. This particular state of mind concentrates all knowledge and intelligence on a single and unique goal.

John Paul Getty

Condition yourself to determine clearly in your mind the goal that you want to achieve, and then, without letting yourself get sidetracked, head straight for your ideal.

Dale Carnegie

If you don't know where you're going, you'll probably end up somewhere else.

L.J. Peter & Raymond Hull

No matter how high or how excellent technology may be and how much capital may be accumulated, unless the group of human beings which comprise the enterprise works together toward one unified goal, the enterprise is sure to go down the path of decline.

Takashi Ishihara

It's not enough to take steps that might one day lead to a goal: each step should, in itself, be a goal, and at the same time carry us closer to a greater goal.

Goethe

I was a newspaper seller, a worker in a printing shop, a toy maker, a glass blower, a delivery boy, etc. But while working at all these occupations, I never lost sight of my final goal, which was to become an author.

Joseph Conrad

When an engineer or researcher has a well-defined goal, he or she works to achieve it. But if the goal is uncertain, and if the company or organization places a large sum of money at his or her disposal and says, 'Go on! Invent something!' then there is no guarantee of success.

Akio Morita

GOD
See also Religion.

Why say, 'I am not Divine?' Remove the word 'not' from the sentence, and see the difference it makes. 'I am Divine.' That is the truth, as far as we are concerned. 'I am not Divine' is a falsehood. The truth is 'I am Divine.' Take that thought to its logical conclusion. 'I am God.'

Baird T. Spalding

I pray to the Almighty to encourage you to dedicate your life to Jesus Christ. Whatever difficulties you may have to face, turn to Him, recognize Him and render Him all your glory, and He will help you overcome.

Colonel Sanders

GOING AGAINST THE CURRENT
See also Innovation; Struggle.

Never forget that only dead fish swim with the stream.

Malcolm Muggeridge

GOLDEN RULE

Do unto others as you would have them do unto you.

Matthew 7:12

The Golden Rule teaches us to 'Do unto others as we would have others do unto us.' The Bible tells us this in the Book of Matthew (7:12), and this message is just as meaningful today as ever. Of course, it was meant for everyone, but what a perfect rule of conduct for people-managers! Unfortunately many people today consider the Golden Rule a tiresome cliché, but it still is the best key to people management. At Mary Kay Cosmetics we take it very seriously. Every people-management decision made is based on the Golden Rule. I truly believe that the Golden Rule was intended to be used seven days a week — not just on Sunday. And that it should be employed in every relationship — business or personal. When you use this rule — every decision becomes a right decision.

Mary Kay Ash

GOODNESS

Good people attract other good people.

Roberto Ruiz

GOVERNMENT

Governments should not interfere in areas where people get along on their own.

Abraham Lincoln

A government can allow itself one year of spending above its means. Same for a household. But you and I both know that making it a habit leads straight to the soup kitchen.

Franklin Roosevelt

I ask nothing from government as long as it doesn't get in my way.

Fred Smith

GREATNESS

There are great men who make everyone feel small. But the real great man is the man who makes every man feel great.

G.K. Chesterton

On the most exalted throne in the world, we are still seated on nothing but our arse.

Michel Eyquem de Montaigne

The greatness of human actions is measured by the extent to which they inspire others.

Louis Pasteur

Great souls are not suspicious; they hide; usually they just seem a little original. There are greater souls among us than we know of.

Stendhal

The characteristic of a great man is his power to leave a lasting impression on people he meets.

Winston Churchill

Real greatness consists of being master of yourself.

Daniel Defoe

Keep away from people who try to belittle your ambitions. Small people always do that. But the really great make you feel that you too can become great.

Mark Twain

To be great is to be misunderstood.

Ralph Waldo Emerson

GREED

People will swim through shit if you put a few dollars in it.

Mark Twain

GROWTH

Every time we acquired a new company we would give a welcoming dinner for the new company's management and we would talk about our goal of at least ten per cent annual growth. It did not make any difference if times were good or bad. When they were good, we should be able to reach our goal easily; when they were bad, we had to work harder. But we had to reach our goal each and every year. That was the message.

Harold Geneen

My way of apprehending business management was very simple. At each stage in the development of Wang Laboratories, I acquired enough knowledge to allow me to lead us to the next stage. Too rapid growth, undertaking projects which are too ambitious, can only lead to disaster. I never really wanted Wang to have an annual growth rate of more than fifty per cent, because I thought I wouldn't be able to direct a company which was developing faster than that. Each challenge met and won gave me more confidence, and made me feel prepared to face even greater challenges in the next step of the growth process.

An Wang

H

HABIT

Changing people's habits costs a lot. A project that includes this condition merits serious reflection. To sell shaving cream to Russian peasants, you'd first have to make them change their habit of wearing beards. That could be too expensive. Yet countless advertisers try to do things which are just as impossible. For the simple reason that they don't take the trouble to consider the realities, and therefore have no control over the results.

Claude C. Hopkins

This image might make you smile, but it is no less efficient for all that. You have to ceaselessly eradicate your weaknesses, which means your tendency to let yourself be taken in by the habits of ordinary men. You only catch the game by knowing its habits; it is easy to defeat a person if you know his habits.

Bernard Tapie

HAPPINESS
See also Contentment.

Happiest are the people who give most happiness to others.

Denis Diderot

The biggest enterprise, and the only one we should take seriously, is to live happily.

Voltaire

Happiness doesn't depend on any external conditions, it is governed by our mental attitude.

Dale Carnegie

Money and time are the heaviest burdens in life: And among mortals, those who are most unhappy are the ones who have more than they need.

Samuel Johnson

One can bear anything, except continual prosperity.

Goethe

Money doesn't make those who don't have any happy.

Boris Vian

Money never prevented anybody from being happy or unhappy.

Eddie Barclay

HASTE

It was not at all my intention to go into production on a mediocre scale. I was thinking big production; but I needed something better than our first car. You don't do anything well if it's done in haste.

Henry Ford

Make haste, but slowly!

Augustus Caesar

HEALTH

All men at the top talk about how hard it is, but take away the pressures inherent in their work, and they'd die.

Fred J. Borch

It's not just by chance that statistics prove that people with elevated incomes live ten years longer than others.

Bernard Tapie

HEART
See also Ambition; Inner Voice.

You have to have your heart in the business and the business in your heart.

Thomas J. Watson Sr

If you want what you're asking me with all your heart, then there's nothing I can do to stop you from getting it.

Andrew Carnegie

A man with heart is someone who remains faithful until there is no more hope. Desperation is cowardice.

Euripides

HESITATION

I never sit on a fence. I am either on one side or another.

Harry S. Truman

HIDDEN TALENT

Most men, like plants, possess hidden properties which they discover by chance.

Duc de la Rochefoucauld

HIRING

All great men are endowed with intuition. A real leader does not need psychological tests or information sheets to choose his subordinates.

Dr Alexis Carrel

Very few great men were hired by the Personnel Department.

Paul Goodman

Hiring someone for a job because he needs it and not because the job needs him is like saying that he is useless. On the other hand, helping a man because it is in our interests to help him is treating him as an equal.

Henry Ford

Here lies a man who knew how to enlist into his service people better than himself.

Andrew Carnegie

I'm just looking to hire the best talent, wherever I can find it.

Donald Trump

I have often compared American companies to constructions of brick, and Japanese ones to constructions of stone. The organization and running of American companies is based on pre-established planning where all tasks are clearly defined. To verify this, just look at the want-ads in any newspaper: the employers establish, for each job offer, a profile of the ideal candidate, and anyone who doesn't fit, either because they aren't good enough or because they're too good, will be systematically eliminated. That's why American companies are made of bricks: each element is made to measure, and must fit perfectly in the whole.

Akio Morita

My conviction is that when you hire a crazy person to do a job, you shouldn't prevent him from acting the way he wants.

Ray Kroc

I never hesitated to promote someone I didn't like. The comfortable assistant — the nice guy you like to go on fishing trips with — is a great pitfall. Instead, I looked for those sharp, scratchy, harsh, almost unpleasant guys who see and tell you about things as they really are. If you can get enough of them around you, and have patience enough to hear them out, there is no limit to where you can go.

Thomas J. Watson, Sr

The importance accorded employees must be sincere, sometimes courageous, even reckless, with no hesitation to take risks. But in time — and time is very important — whatever your capacities are, whatever your successes, your shrewdness, your dexterity, the future of your business is in the hands of the people you have hired.

Akio Morita

HOBBIES

Every young man should have a hobby. Learning how to handle money is the best one.

Jack Hurley

HUMAN RELATIONS
See also Personnel.

If the only tool you have is a hammer, you treat everything like a nail.

Abraham Maslow

When I take stock of life, I realize how important the personal contact is, how much more they are worth than the invention of machines, because [people] allow us to expand our view of things, and open up thousands of experiences which we would otherwise be unable to understand.

Soichiro Honda

Be genuinely interested in people. Remember, every person — be he duke or beggar — has some unique experiences. You encourage them to talk about themselves and their families; wherever you can, you should do the listening rather than the talking. Where conversation flags you can always ask a sympathetic question or make a provocative statement. A great deal of experience in life can be obtained by observing closely the behaviour and actions and reactions of other human beings, measuring their conduct against your own and deciding the standards that you wish to observe and making certain that you do so.

Robert Maxwell

HUNGER

I was like a hungry man who had to listen to long explanations of dietary laws and their effects instead of being given something to eat.

Soichiro Honda

I

IDEALISM

An idealist is a person who helps others prosper.

Henry Ford

IDEAS

One sound idea is all that you need to achieve success.

Napoleon Hill

As soon as an idea is accepted, it is time to reject it.

Holbrook Jackson

I work from details outward to the general, and I don't stop developing big ideas until I have worked out the minutest detail.

Ray Kroc

Each worker is considered as a source of ideas and not just as a pair of arms.

Mark Shepherd

The key is to go into the store and listen to what the employees have to say. Because our best ideas come from them.

Sam Walton

The majority of businesspeople are incapable of having an original idea because they can not free themselves from the restraints of logic.

David Ogilvy

The best way to have a good idea is to have a lot of ideas.

Linus Pauling

Take any giant corporation, and I'm talking about the big ones, and you'll find that they were all started by one person who had a good idea and knew how to exploit it.

Irvine Robbins

Ideas, ideas, that's what we need.

Helena Rubinstein

I have found that ideas come when you have a great desire to find them; the mind becomes a kind of watchtower from which we look out for any incident that might excite the imagination; music, a sunset, etc., can germinate an idea.

Charlie Chaplin

The best way to exploit your ideas is to act in concert with your colleagues. That's why I advocate frequent managerial meetings. Not always 'work sessions' with an official stamp, just simple conversations on an informal basis where we exchange information and ideas that can help us solve problems faster.

Lee Iacocca

Most good ideas sparkle in simplicity, so much so that everyone wonders why no one ever did that before.

Estée Lauder

How do we get ideas? Through perseverance, pushed to the point of madness. You have to be able to deal with anxiety and to maintain your enthusiasm for a long period of time. Maybe it's easier for some than for others, but I doubt it.

Charlie Chaplin

IMAGINATION

Imagination is more important than knowledge.

Albert Einstein

I force myself not to lack imagination.

Marcel Dassault

IMITATION
See also Innovation.

Replicate, don't innovate . . ... Someone else has gone and done your homework for you. They have taken the risk, the time, and spent the dollars.

Steven W. Lapham

A good composer does not imitate, he steals.

Igor Stravinsky

IMPETUS

You may instigate the first action in business, but after that it drives you along.

Napoleon Bonaparte

IMPOSSIBLE

How often have I said to you that when you have eliminated the impossible, whatever remains, however improbable, must be the truth?

Arthur Conan Doyle

Difficult things take time: impossible things take a little more time.

Chaim Weizmann

My engineer's calculations are clear: the project is impossible. There's only one thing left for us to do: get on with the project.

Père Latecoere

I love those who reach for the impossible.

Goethe

I refuse to recognize the existence of impossibilities. I don't know anyone who knows enough about any subject to be able to say that something is or is not impossible. If someone who takes himself for an expert and declares that such and such a thing is impossible, right away there's a horde of nincompoops who sing the chorus: 'It's impossible ...'

Henry Ford

Usually, most people I know disagree with almost all the projects, but when I announced my intention to buy and build at Revolcadero Beach, the reaction was for once unanimous: Impossible! The reasons they found to judge my project impossible were legion — and I must admit for the most part reasonable. Still, I thought — I knew — that the project could be done. When opening day came around, the luxury hotel was everything I had wanted it to be, and its instant success surpassed even my own expectations. Here was another impossible project that became 100 per cent possible right from the start. There are and will be many others — small and large — before and after.

John Paul Getty

When I started making motorcycles, the prophets of doom, some of them my friends, came to discourage me. 'You'd be better off opening another garage, in the country or in Tokyo. You'll make a lot of money. There are a lot of cars that need to be repaired in this country.' I didn't listen to them, and despite their pessimistic advice I created, on the 24th of September, 1948, next door to my research laboratory, the Honda Motor Company, which today is successful around the world.

Soichiro Honda

'It's impossible,' you write; I don't understand ... that's not French!

Napoleon Bonaparte

He didn't know that it was impossible, so he did it.

Jean Cocteau

INCLINATION

It is good to follow your path, provided you are on the way up!

André Gide

INCOMPETENCE

It is not the crook in modern business that we fear, but the honest man who does not know what he is doing.

Owen D. Young

The Peter Principle: In a hierarchy, every employee tends to rise to his or her level of greatest incompetence. Work is accomplished by those employees who have not yet reached their level of incompetence. Competence, like truth, beauty and contact lenses, is in the eye of the beholder.

L.J. Peter & Raymond Hull

Every incompetent director is surrounded with assistants who are just as incompetent.

Lee Iacocca

INDIFFERENCE

Look at that worm on the ground, there on the ground. If I step on it, I draw attention to it. If I ignore it, it disappears.

John Rockefeller

INDISPENSABLE

If you know how to make yourself indispensable to a client, you will never get fired.

David Ogilvy

The graveyards are full of indispensable men.

Charles de Gaulle

An organization with an indispensable man is guilty of management failure.

Harold S. Hook

INDIVIDUALITY

When two businessmen always agree, one of them is useless.

William Wrigley

It would not be a good thing if everyone thought the same way: It's the differences in opinion that make the race interesting.

Mark Twain

INDUSTRIALISTS

The world has expected a lot more from industrialists who love their work than from founders of hospitals.

Alfred North Whitehead

INDUSTRY
See also 'Work Smarts'.

It is not enough to be industrious: so are ants. What are you industrious about?

Henry David Thoreau

The busier we are, the more acutely we feel that we live, the more conscious we are of life.

Immanuel Kant

The hardest job of all is trying to look busy when you're not.

George Coleman

INFLATION

Inflation is the only tax that can be raised without the law.

Milton Friedman

INFORMATION

The secret of business is to be the only one in possession of certain information.

Aristotle Onassis

For an organization to function well, information must flow along the most efficient channel, whatever that may be.

David Packard

The main problem encountered by American heads of business is that they have to deal with too much information. This confuses them, and they end up not knowing what to do.

Lee Iacocca

A man's opinions are less valuable than the information he gathers.

John Paul Getty

The second best thing, after being familiar with a subject, is knowing where to find the information concerning that subject.

Samuel Johnson

INHERITANCE

I really do not see why someone who is dying would leave an amount of half a million or a million dollars to his successors when he knows that an immense percentage will go to taxes. That's why I gave my Canadian subsidiary to a charitable foundation. The other reason, as I have said, is that I wanted to do something for God.

Colonel Sanders

The meek shall inherit the earth, but not the mineral rights.

John Paul Getty

When you have informed someone that you are leaving them an inheritance, the only decent thing left for you to do is to die as quickly as possible.

Samuel Butler

INJUSTICE

The feeling of injustice can give a person incredible force. No other feeling, neither hate, nor resentment, can give a person the energy he lacks. I never wanted revenge on my adversaries; I just ignored them. I absolutely had to prove that I was not what they thought I was, what they tried to force me to be: It's through this rebellion against the limits that others want to impose on you that you overtake them, turning failure into indestructible powerful success.

Bernard Tapie

INNER VOICE
See also Ambition; Heart.

Each businessperson must find a style, that voice that grows clearer and louder with each success and failure. Observing your own and your competitors' successes and failures makes your inner business voice more sure and vivid.

Estée Lauder

INNOVATION
See also Creativity.

Business has two basic functions — marketing and innovation.

Peter Drucker

You see how things are, and you ask 'Why?' But I dream of things that do not yet exist, and I ask 'Why not?'

George Bernard Shaw

A perspicacious businessperson clings to the old as long as it is good, and seizes the new as soon as it is better.

Robert Vanderpoel

If you want to succeed, you have to forge new paths and avoid borrowed ones that promise success.

John Rockefeller

INSTINCT
See also Faith.

One point is to listen to your gut, no matter how good something sounds on paper. The second is that you're generally better off sticking with what you know. And the third is that sometimes your best investments are the ones you don't make.

Donald Trump

The most precious thing I have is a kind of clairvoyance that gives me the certitude that my projects are not crazy, that it would, on the contrary, be crazy not to undertake them. My instinct has not let me down up to now, and so I tried hard to create this foundation and find the money.

Claude Bourg

INTELLIGENCE

Work smarter, not harder.

Allan Morgensen & Lillian Gilbreth

INTUITION

The final touch to business judgment is, of course, intuition.

Alfred Sloan

Your sixth sense can warn you in time of imminent dangers so that you can avoid them, and of good opportunities so that you can take advantage of them.

Napoleon Hill

No matter how deep a study you made, what you really have to rely on is your own intuition and when it comes down to it, you really don't know what's going to happen until you do it.

Konosuke Matsushita

People who find themselves heading a company not only have to know their business, but also their environment; they have to be able to take calculated risks based on their knowledge, and also based on what is called the 'sixth sense.' I hope the readers will not find me too vain when I remind them that it was my intuition that convinced me the *Walkman* would be a great success, and in a published article I expressed my conviction despite the scepticism my idea was met with. In it I said ... 'If we haven't sold 100,000 *Walkmans* from now to the end of the year, I will resign from my position as President of the company.' I had no intention of resigning, obviously; but I just knew that this device would be a success.

Akio Morita

The first task of a company director is to make decisions. This requires the right professional qualifications, solid technical knowledge and a feel for where technology is going. A company director, in my opinion, should have wide general knowledge in addition to his professional background. This is indispensable for sharpening that particular gift, the fruit of knowledge and experience — a business sense which goes beyond numbers alone — I'm talking about intuition, the privilege of human beings alone.

Akio Morita

I am a visceral person by nature. I act on instinct, quickly, without pondering possible disaster and without indulging in deep introspection.

Estée Lauder

INVENTION

Everything a man has created or invented was first a thought in his mind, a clearly formulated idea in his mind, before taking the form of an objective, exterior entity.

Dr J. Murphy

INVESTING

Buy land — it is not made any more these days.

Mark Twain

Invest in inflation — it is the only thing that keeps going up.

Will Rogers

The best investment on earth is earth.

Louis Glickman

Nothing is more disastrous than a rational investment in an irrational world.

John Maynard Keynes

All businesses that fall flat on their faces have at least one point in common; over the years, they did not make a single investment.

Bernard Tapie

IRREPLACEABLE

Don't be irreplaceable. If you can't be replaced, you can't be promoted.

Anonymous

J

JAPANESE

We were fairly arrogant, until we realized the Japanese were selling quality products for what it cost us to make them.

Paul A. Allaire

The Japanese employ open discussions with generalities that leave room for movement and compromise. They have nineteen ways of saying no—suggestive of the extreme finesse with which their language navigates the shoals of conflict, avoiding it if possible.

Richard T. Pascale

Fifty percent of Japanese companies do not have a marketing department, and ninety percent have no special section for marketing research. The reason is that everyone is considered to be a marketing specialist.

Hirotaka Takeuchi

JUDGING

Judge a man by his questions rather than by his answers.

Voltaire

JUMPING IN
See also Perserverance.

All of our senior executives, including me, knew what it felt like to be thrown into deep water not knowing if you could swim.

Thomas J. Watson Sr

The business of life is to go forward.

Samuel Johnson

The best thing that can happen to nine out of ten young people is to get pushed into the water and to have to learn how to swim, even if the water is sometimes ice cold.

James Abram Garfield

Henceforth I went to school every morning, and in the evening when I came home I would practise what I'd learned in my little studio. I forced myself to be enthusiastic. But I had no choice, and when you place yourself in situations where there are no alternatives, a kind of freedom is born in you, the freedom that comes from a decision you made from which there is no turning back. A thousand reasons to persevere filled my mind. Friends had placed their confidence in me, and my father too, as well as all the men who worked with me. I no longer had the right to go back, and only school could get me what I wanted — to become an engineer, to be able to theorize my technological intuition and assure production. I solemnly said to myself: If I give up now, everyone will die of hunger. And I imagined the pathetic state of all those people who were depending on me.

Soichiro Honda

Take time to deliberate, but when the time for action has arrived, stop thinking and jump in.

Napoleon Bonaparte

K

KEEPING YOUR HEAD

If you can keep your head while all about you are losing
theirs and blaming it on you ... yours is the Earth and
everything that's in it, and — which is more — you'll be a
Man, my son!

Rudyard Kipling

KEY TO SUCCESS
See also Winning Formulas.

The man who puts all his energy and imagination into
finding ways to offer more for the dollar instead of less is
condemned to succeed.

Henry Ford

KNACK FOR BUSINESS

I really had the knack for business. My mind was
constantly occupied with schemes and projects: if I saw
some empty shops, I would always ask myself what kind
of profitable business I could open — from selling fish and
chips to groceries.

Charlie Chaplin

KNOWLEDGE
See also Wisdom.

Superior people know everything without having learned anything.

Molière

We should concentrate on the things we know best.

Arthur Spear

We have never strayed from our original field. We want everything, except to become a conglomerate.

Edward G. Harness

Nothing in the world is more dangerous than sincere ignorance and conscientious stupidity.

Martin Luther King

We don't even know about one millionth of one per cent of what exists.

Thomas A. Edison

If, in a limited group, there are intelligent people who know themselves well, then problems will be resolved one way or another.

Jim Burke

I learn things every day.

Philip Morris

Working a lot, and learning from your work, is the best thing you can do.

Richard Braddock

I can learn a lot more from going door to door for three hours than from sitting in my office for three years.

William J. Bresman

The more one knows about a person, the greater one's power to destroy him.

Stanley I. Benn

L

LAUGHTER

It seems you can know a man by his laugh, and if on first meeting a stranger he laughs in a friendly and agreeable way, you can conclude that the rest is excellent.

Fïodor Dostoïevski

Try to make working at Ogilvy and Mather fun. When people aren't having any fun, they seldom produce good advertising. Kill grimness with laughter. Maintain an atmosphere of informality. Encourage exuberance. Get rid of sad dogs that spread gloom.

David Ogilvy

LAWSUITS

To Messrs Morgan and Garrison: Gentlemen, you have undertaken to cheat me. I will not sue you. The law takes too long. I will ruin you.

Cornelius Vanderbilt

LAWYERS
See also Accountants.

I don't want a lawyer who tells me what I can't do. I hire a lawyer to tell me how I can do what I want.

J.P. Morgan

Lawyers earn a living trying to understand what other lawyers have written.

Will Rogers

LAZINESS

I do not like work, even when someone else does it.

Mark Twain

Laziness is nothing more than the habit of resting before you get tired.

Jules Renard

Work is the greatest thing in the world, so we should always save some of it for tomorrow.

Don Herold

Hard work never killed anybody, but why take a chance.

Charlie McCarthy

Lazy people don't live long.

Rose Blumkin

There is no pleasure in having nothing to do. The fun is having lots to do, and not doing it.

John W. Raper

Be lazy enough to find someone to do the work for you. You have to take time out to think.

Meshulam Riklis

I have succeeded in reducing my working time to thirty minutes. That leaves me eighteen hours a day to keep busy.

Charles Steinmetz

I believe that each individual has a limited number of heartbeats. And I have no intention of wasting a single one on running or exercise.

Neil Armstrong

Laziness, rather than necessity, is often the mother of invention.

Robert Noyce

I never liked to work, I mean manual work; as for head work, on the contrary, I have always enjoyed it, and have always combined my mental pleasure with making money. But manual labour, I repeat, was always distasteful, so while my father considered that I was as suitable as the next person to weed, plough and hoe the garden, I always found ways to get out of the work I was given, or to do it badly.

P.T. Barnum

LEADERSHIP
See also Power.

When the best leader's work is done the people say, 'We did it ourselves.'

Lao-Tzu

Show me a country or a company that is not doing well and I'll show you a bad leader.

Joseph E. Brooks

Love those you command. But don't tell them.

Antoine de Saint-Exupéry

Leadership can not really be taught. It can only be learned.

Harold Geneen

A strong person (or two) is almost always the cause of success in the best companies.

Thomas Peters & Robert Waterman

A leader has to take people from where they are to where they have never been before.

Henry Kissinger

Whoever accepts mediocrity is a person who makes compromises. And when the leader makes a compromise, the rest of the company does too.

Charles Knight d'Emerson

To my mind, the quality of leadership is the single most important ingredient in the recipe for business success.

Harold Geneen

The big boss should be more Catholic than the Pope.

Robert McNamara

The superior leader gets things done with very little motion. He imparts instruction not through many words but through a few deeds. He keeps informed about everything but interferes hardly at all. He is a catalyst, and though things would not get done as well if he weren't there, when they succeed he takes no credit. And because he takes no credit, credit never leaves him.

Lao-Tzu

Managers prefer to work with people, while leaders arouse emotion in people.

Abraham Zalisnick, Business Psychologist

The speed of the leader is the speed of the gang.

Mary Kay Ash

What you should show your employees is not the great artist you are, balancing on a tightrope, but the part of you that is capable of attracting the greatest number of people, and instilling in them the desire to follow you with enthusiasm and contribute to the success of the enterprise. When you get results like these, the last in line follow the lead of those in front.

Akio Morita

I start with the premise that the function of leadership is to produce more leaders, not more followers.

Ralph Nader

As for the best leaders, the people do not notice their existence. The next best, the people honour and praise. The next, the people fear; and the next, the people hate.

Lao-Tzu

LEARNING FROM OTHERS

Who deserves to be called wise? He who finds something to learn from each person.

Mishna

LIKES AND DISLIKES

One of our ironclad rules is 'Never do business with anybody you don't like.' If you don't like somebody, there's a reason. Chances are it's because you don't trust him, and you're probably right. I don't care who it is or what guarantees you get — cash in advance or whatever. If you do business with somebody you don't like, sooner or later you'll get screwed.

Henry V. Quadracci

I liked the shaver so much that I bought the company.

Victor Kiam

LIKING YOUR WORK
See also Love; Pleasure.

From as early as I can remember, my father would say to me, 'The most important thing in life is to love what you're doing, because that's the only way you'll ever be really good at it.'

Donald Trump

The sound of the machine was my first music. From the veranda of our wooden house, I could see the blue smoke it emitted. One day I asked my grandfather to take me there. It became a habit. I always loved the smell of oil permeating everything, the noise of the combustion motors, the smoke ...and I stayed there for hours, watching the machine while my grandfather tried to talk me into going back.

Soichiro Honda

I believed in my product. I loved my product. I loved to touch the creams, smell them, look at them, carry them with me. A person has to love her harvest if she's to expect others to love it. And beauty was such a bountiful harvest.

Estée Lauder

Work that you find interesting is never hard, and will certainly lead to success.

Henry Ford

LIMITS

There are no limitations to the mind except those we acknowledge.

Napoleon Hill

Man lives well below his limits. He possesses powers of all kinds which he generally does not use at all.

William James

LISTENING

Remember a listener is always more appreciated than a talker and avoid boasting. On the other hand, one must not fall into the other scale of being too self-effacing or too frightened to intervene in a conversation.

Robert Maxwell

The one that listens is the one that understands.

Anonymous

It is as important for a good manager to know how to listen as well as to talk. We too often forget that communication is an exchange.

Lee Iacocca

LOVE
See also Liking Your Work; Pleasure.

Never forget that the most powerful force on earth is love.

Nelson Rockefeller

Let's take the hamburger bun, for example. You have to have a certain kind of mind to find beauty in these buns. On the other hand, is it any stranger to find beauty in the texture and gentle curves of a hamburger bun than to think affectionately of the design of a fishing fly or the delicate colors of a butterfly wing? Not if you're a McDonald's man. Not if you look at the hamburger bun as an essential element in the art of serving a large number of meals quickly and efficiently. So this little mass of dough becomes an object worthy of serious study.

Ray Kroc

LOSS

Show me a good loser and I'll show you an idiot.

Leo Durocher

Show me a good loser and I'll show you a loser.

Wallace 'Chief' Newman

The minute you start talking about what you're going to do if you lose, you have lost.

George Schultz

LUCK
See also Circumstance; Destiny; Events

I still believe that my first successes were due to pure luck.

John Paul Getty

We have to believe in luck. If not, how can we explain the success of people we don't like!

Jean Cocteau

It's far from easy to make profit: luck and circumstance play an incredibly important role in success.

Bernard Tapie

Luck always seems to find those who know how to use it.

Romain Rolland

. . . lucky you will say, but luck only favors the mind which is prepared.

Louis Pasteur

The harder you work, the luckier you get.

Gary Player

People do make their luck by daring to follow their instincts, taking risks, and embracing every possibility.

Estée Lauder

LUNCH

Eat moderately; when you have something urgent to take care of, avoid rich foods and wine. Spending hours at the table, while your mind is wrapped up in work that has to be done, is still one of the best ways to shorten your existence.

Aristotle Onassis

I worked every day from nine, when I arrived to polish my jars, to six in the evening. I never lunched.

Estée Lauder

I ask my executive assistant and the person who keeps my life organized, to bring me lunch: a can of tomato juice. I rarely go out, because mostly it's a waste of time.

Donald Trump

LURE OF GAIN
See also Money.

I spent my whole life working for charity. Now I work for money. It's just as much fun.

Charlotte Ford

People who are willing to work for nothing worry me, because that's usually what they do for you — nothing.

Sam Ervin

M

MACHINES

The factory of the future will have only two employees, a man and a dog. The man will be there to feed the dog. The dog will be there to keep the man from touching the equipment.

Warren G. Bennis

It is said that one machine can do the work of fifty ordinary men. No machine, however, can do the work of one extraordinary man.

Tehyi Hsieh

Machines should work. People should think.

John Peers

Men have become the tools of their tools.

Henry David Thoreau

The enemy of the marketplace is not ideology, but the machine.

John Kenneth Galbraith

MADNESS

The reasonable man adapts himself to the world; the unreasonable one persists in trying to adapt the world to himself. Therefore all progress depends on the unreasonable man.

George Bernard Shaw

MAGNETISM

Our brains become magnetized with the dominating thoughts which we store in them and, through a process which no one understands, these thoughts, like magnets, attract forces, people, and life circumstances which harmonize with them.

Napoleon Hill

MANAGEMENT
See also Collaboration; Co-operation; Motivation.

The ability to handle people is a commodity that can be bought like sugar and coffee, and I'm ready to pay more for this ability than for any other on earth.

John Rockefeller

I don't believe in just ordering people to do things. You have to sort of grab an oar and row with them. My philosophy is to stay as close as possible to what is happening. If I can't solve something, how the hell can I expect my managers to do it?

Harold Geneen

If you don't drive your business, you will be driven out of business.

B.C. Forbes

Lots of folks confuse bad management with destiny.

Frank McKinney Hubbard

Much of present-day management — MBAs or the equivalent — are perhaps a little too intelligent, but the people who direct the best companies are a little simplistic.

Thomas Peters and Robert Waterman

A good manager is a man who isn't worried about his own career, but rather the careers of those who work for him. My advice: don't worry about yourself. Take care of those who work for you, and you will float to greatness on their achievements.

H.S.M. Burns

Management consists of showing average people how to produce superior work.

John Rockefeller

I don't like managing personnel to think they belong to some kind of special species favoured by the gods, in charge of guiding stupid people towards a kind of miraculous revelation which will confirm certain peculiarities in the business world.

Akio Morita

Nine out of ten businesses fail because of bad management.

Joseph W. Duncan

The main objective of management should be to assure the employer's optimum prosperity, combined with the optimum prosperity of each employee.

Frederick W. Taylor

In terms of business management, the minimum has the maximum effect.

Ray Kroc

I believe in the notion of management as a good father runs his family.

Marcel Bich

Make your managers rich, and they will make you rich.

Robert W. Johnson

Management must manage!

Harold Geneen

American management is not interested enough in its workers.

Akio Morita

When we say that someone 'manages' we imply that he follows an obligatory path which is already established. But this is not the case. I am convinced that managing means controlling the steering wheel and driving the company in the best possible direction, as fast as possible and without mishap.

Jean-Luc Lagardère

In my opinion, the qualities of a good manager consist of being able to organize the activities of a large number of individuals, and meld them together so that their efforts are well co-ordinated.

Akio Morita

What you manage in business is people.

Harold Geneen

In today's management, I absolutely do not believe in authority imposed by a hierarchy; decisions must be made, that's obvious, but I want the team around me to be as responsible as I am, as motivated, as united in controlling our destiny as myself, and that seems to me absolutely fundamental.

Bernard Tapie

To be a manager, you have to start at the bottom — no exceptions.

Henry Block

Aspirin doctor: A manager who tries to solve every problem the same way, like a doctor who prescribes aspirin for every unknown illness.

Harold S. Hook

My most important contribution to IBM was my ability to pick strong and intelligent men and then hold the team together by persuasion, by apologies, by financial incentives, by speeches, by chatting with their wives, by thoughtfulness when they were sick or involved in an accident, and by using every tool at my command to make that team think that I was a decent guy. I knew I couldn't match all of them intellectually, but I thought that if I fully used every capability that I had, I could stay even with them.

Thomas J. Watson Sr

Key men in key positions!

John Rockefeller

Treat people as if they were who they could be, and you will help them become what they are capable of becoming.

Goethe

MARKETPLACE

Twenty-four out of twenty-five products do not survive the test of the marketplace.

David Ogilvy

Some people have a sense of the market and some people don't. Steven Spielberg has it. Lee Iacocca of Chrysler has it, and so does Judith Krantz in her way. Woody Allen has it for the audience he cares about reaching, and so does Sylvester Stallone, at the other end of the spectrum. Some people criticize Stallone, but you've got to give him credit. I mean, here's a man who is just 41 years old, and he's already created two of the all-time great characters, Rocky and Rambo. To me he's a diamond-in-the-rough type, a genius purely by instinct. He knows what the public wants and he delivers it.

Donald Trump

MASTER OF BUSINESS ADMINISTRATION
See also Diplomas; Education; School.

You don't need an MBA from Harvard to figure out how to lose money.

Royal Little

MEASURE FOR MEASURE

There is a measure to all things, and knowing how to seize its meaning is the foremost science.

Themistocles

MEDIOCRITY

Only a mediocre person is always at his best.

Laurence Peter

Mediocrity knows nothing higher than itself, but talent instantly recognizes genius.

Arthur Conan Doyle

MEETINGS

One of the rules in our meetings is that you can ask someone to clarify their thoughts, but not to explain them because that would take all day.

William G. McGowan

If a problem causes many meetings, the meetings eventually become more important than the problem.

Arthur Bloch

Don't call a meeting in your office — it scares people. Go and see them in their offices.

David Ogilvy

No grand idea was ever born in a conference, but a lot of foolish ideas have died there.

F. Scott Fitzgerald

I have at least a dozen meetings. The majority occur on the spur of the moment, and few of them last longer than fifteen minutes.

Donald Trump

MEN
See also Women.

It is a general mistake to think that the men we like are good for everything, and those we do not, good for nothing.

George Savile

Anyone who critically analyzes a business learns this: that success or failure of an enterprise usually depends on one man.

Louis D. Brandeis

MENTALITY
See also Ambition.

Luck, knowledge and arduous work — especially arduous work — are all necessary for a man to become a millionaire. But, above all that, he needs what can be called the 'millionaire mentality': that essential state of mind and conscience which mobilizes the intelligence and all the talents of an individual to accomplish his tasks and realize the goals he has set for himself in business.

John Paul Getty

MERCENARY

Mercenary captains may or may not be very capable men. If they are, you can't trust them, because they'll always do what's good for them, even if it means betraying you, their master, or using other people against their will. And if the captain is not capable, he will ruin you.

Machiavelli

MERIT

Remember that everything that happens has a just cause. You will understand this if your observations are accurate. I'm not just saying one thing leads to another, but one thing leads justly to another, as if someone assigned each person the merit he deserved. Continue observing, and whatever you do, do it with this thought in mind, the thought of being a good man, according to the accepted ideas of what constitutes a good man. Apply this principle to all your actions.

Marcus Aurelius

MILLIONAIRES
See also Billionaires.

There's a lot of room at the top. This symbolic Millionaire's Club has an unlimited number of vacant seats to fill on its membership roster. I'm afraid that if theses seats are not filled more quickly, it is because young potential candidates, who are very qualified, give up the fight before it really begins.

John Paul Getty

I am a Millionaire. That is my religion.

George Bernard Shaw

MIND

All things are ready when the mind is ready.

William Shakespeare

Whatever the mind of man can conceive and believe, it can achieve.

Napoleon Hill

One man that has a mind and knows it can always beat ten men who haven't and don't.

George Bernard Shaw

All things are ready, if our minds be so.

William Shakespeare

No two minds ever come together without thereby creating a third, invisible, intangible force which may be likened to a third, or master mind. Analyse the record of any man who has accumulated a great fortune, and many of those who have accumulated modest fortunes, and you will find that they have either consciously or unconsciously employed the 'Master Mind' principle.

Napoleon Hill

MIXING BUSINESS WITH PLEASURE

I do not know what I may appear to the world; but to myself I seem to have been only like a boy playing on the seashore, and diverting myself in now and then finding a smoother pebble or a prettier shell than ordinary, whilst the great ocean of truth lay all undiscovered before me.

Isaac Newton

Every person gets his pleasure from the instrument he plays best.

Henri-René Lenormand

A man cannot succeed in a difficult task unless he takes pleasure in doing it.

Anonymous

Business is more exciting than any game.

Lord Beaverbrook

Men try to keep women out of business because they don't want us to find out how much fun it is.

Vivien Kellems

Arrange your business so people can take pleasure in working for you. When your employees are bored, they rarely do good work.

David Ogilvy

It is impossible to do anything well without pleasure.

Charles Knight d'Emerson

Taking calculated risks is part of the challenge. It is a pleasurable activity.

Ray Kroc

I never took pleasure in earning money. Money is not necessarily related to happiness. Maybe it is related to unhappiness.

John Paul Getty

The only thing that gives me pleasure is to watch the dividends fall.

John Rockefeller

The thrill, believe me, is as much in the battle as in the victory.

David Sarnoff

MODESTY

Humility is the waiting room to all perfection.

Marcel Ayme

No modest man ever did or ever will make a fortune.

Lady Mary Wortley Montagu

MONEY
See also Circulation; Lure of Gain; Profit; Riches.

He that is of the opinion that money will do everything may well be suspected of doing anything for money.

Benjamin Franklin

It is a kind of spiritual snobbery that makes people think they can be happy without money.

Albert Camus

Money can say more in one moment than the most eloquent lover can in years.

Henry Fielding

Money is like an arm or a leg — use it or lose it.

Henry Ford

Money is always around, it just changes hands. That's all that can be said about it.

Gertrude Stein

Money is the religion of the wise.

Euripides

Money is a pitiless master, but a zealous servant.

P.T. Barnum

Money is the rose of life. One never talks about it without making excuses. However, its effect and its logic imbue it with the beauty of a rose.

Ralph Waldo Emerson

It always interests me to see thousands and millions of dollars bouncing around on a piece of paper.

Joseph. R. Mancuso

If you don't know the price of money, go try and borrow some.

Benjamin Franklin

Money gives an appearance of beauty even to ugliness; but everything becomes frightful with poverty.

Boileau

Money is like fertilizer. You have to spread it around everywhere, if not it stinks.

John Paul Getty

Money is like a sixth sense, indispensable for the proper functioning of the other five.

W. Somerset Maugham

Money is the credit card of the poor.

Marshall McLuhan

I'd like to live like a poor man, but with a lot of money.

Pablo Picasso

It takes more than money to make a business a success.

Mary Kay Ash

People who say that money isn't everything in life are usually broke.

Malcolm Forbes

The first buck is a bit more difficult to earn than the second million.

Jean-Jacques Rousseau

Lack of money is a cruel deprivation, while, past a certain point, an excess of money means nothing.

Bernard Tapie

Business? It's quite simple: it's other people's money.

Alexander Dumas the Younger

I made a resolution to let my money work instead of me!

John Rockefeller

Money is just an allowance.

Coco Chanel

I recall what Maxine Elliot, a friend of J.P. Morgan, told me one day: 'Money is only useful so you can forget it.' But personally, I think it's also something you have to remember.

Charlie Chaplin

Everybody has some, nobody has enough. You hate it when it's lacking, but you welcome it with open arms. We resent having to discuss it, but we think about it all the time. It is the lifeblood of economy, the all-purpose tool, the instrument of success. It heals, it makes people sick, it saves, it kills. It sleeps, it circulates, it fertilizes, it disappears, it corrupts, it grows, it changes hands. It is merited, and it's dirty. We use it, dream about it, hide it, exhibit it, lose it, waste it, disdain it, adore it. We accumulate it like a treasure, but then it becomes sterile. We meditate on it, renounce it, envy it. People use it to reflect their intimate desires, their rivalries, successes, frustrations, ambitions and resentments. At night it rises up, takes form, dominates our thoughts, illuminates, protects, crushes. It is a phantom god whom we implore and resist. It is the scapegoat for all the problems we face. It is a universal commodity, embellished with the whole range of human emotions; it is the measure of our existence.

Guy de Rothschild

One simply cannot start from zero. If you want to start your own business, save some money or know someone who can lend you some. You may not need a huge amount, but those first bills must be covered — and then some. When I began, business practice was based on CBD — Cash *Before* Delivery — not COD [Cash On Delivery]. The same holds true in many cases today.

Estée Lauder

Money is a wonderful commodity to have, but the more one possesses, the more involved and complicated become his dealings and relationships with people.

John Paul Getty

MOTIVATION
See also Collaboration; Co-operation; Management

I consider my ability to arouse enthusiasm in people as my most precious capital asset. It is by encouraging an individual that you can awaken and develop his best qualities.

Charles Schwab

Help other people get what they want — and you'll get what you want.

Mary Kay Ash

The natural first step is to instil the idea that the undertaking is at the same time important and practically impossible ... that is what unleashes the motivation that produces strong men.

Edwin H. Land

There is only one way under high heaven to get anybody to do anything. Did you ever stop to think of that? Yes, just one way. And that is by motivating the other person to want to do it. Remember, there is no other way.

Dale Carnegie

All you need is to tell a man he is no good ten times a day, and very soon he begins to believe it himself.

Lin Yutang

Every person is special! I sincerely believe this. Each of us wants to feel good about himself or herself, but to me it is just as important to make others feel the same way. Whenever I meet someone, I try to imagine him wearing an invisible sign that says: *Make Me Feel Important!* I respond to this sign immediately, and it works wonders.

Mary Kay Ash

What industry has taught us in terms of relations with people is that they don't work just to make money; if you want to motivate them, money is not the best means. To motivate people, you have to make them feel part of a family and treat them with the respect due to members of a family.

Akio Morita

The only way to motivate people is to communicate with them.

Lee Iacocca

Three people were at work on a construction site. All were doing the same job, but when each was asked what his job was, the answers varied. 'Breaking rocks', the first replied. 'Earning my living', the second said. 'Helping to build a cathedral', said the third.

Peter Schultz

N

NAIVETÉ

There's a sucker born every minute.

P.T. Barnum

NECESSITY

Necessity is the mother of invention.

Plato

I would think of another fundamental need people have, and I would answer that need by offering a cheaper and more efficient service than anybody else could. In five years, I'd be a millionaire all over again.

Henry Ford

The most important justification for being in business is service to others. Every new business must be built upon the premise, since wanting to make money or desiring to 'dabble' in a favorite pastime are not enough to sustain such a venture. The business must fulfil a need.

Mary Kay Ash

NEGOTIATION
See also Deals; Strategy.

Arrange it so that the conquered feel glad to have you as their conqueror.

Lao-Tzu

Information is a negotiator's greatest weapon.

Victor Kiam

My style of deal-making is quite simple and straightforward. I aim very high, and then I just keep pushing and pushing and pushing to get what I'm after. Sometimes I settle for less than I sought, but in most cases I still end up with what I want.

Donald Trump

NOBLESSE

A peculiarity of man is to be able to love even those who cause him harm. The way to do this is to consider these people as your parents; that they sin through ignorance, against their will; that soon you'll all be dead anyway; and most importantly, that they really haven't caused you any harm, since they haven't been able to damage your guiding principles.

Marcus Aurelius

NUMBERS

Ultimately, vision gets translated into sales and profit, growth and return on investment, but the numbers come after the vision. In the old-style companies, the numbers are the vision.

John Naisbett

The drudgery of the numbers will make you free.

Harold Geneen

Learn to make numbers talk! They will speak to you about hard truths and also reveal the future!

John Rockefeller

As an accountant by profession, and an old-fashioned bookkeeper at heart, I have always believed that numbers are the bare bones of a corporation.

Harold Geneen

O

OBJECTIVITY

You've got to think about 'big things' while you're doing small things, so that all the small things go in the right direction.

Alvin Toffler

OBSESSION
See also Single-mindedness.

Nothing great is ever achieved without an obsession, that nail which pierces the invisible.

Malcolm de Chazal

Nothing extraordinary, great or beautiful is ever accomplished without thinking about it more often and better than others.

King Louis XIV

One of the keys to thinking big is total focus. I think of it almost as a controlled neurosis, which is a quality I've noticed in many highly successful entrepreneurs. They're obsessive, they're driven, they're single-minded and sometimes they're almost maniacal, but it's all channelled into their work. Where other people are paralysed by neurosis, the people I'm talking about are actually helped by it.

Donald Trump

OBSTACLES
See also Determination; Opportunity; Positive Thinking.

The inner master, when confronted with an obstacle, uses it as fuel, like a fire which consumes things that are thrown into it. A small lamp would be snuffed out, but a big fire will engulf what is thrown at it and burn hotter; it consumes the obstacle and uses it to reach a higher level.

Marcus Aurelius

I really don't work at my best unless there are obstacles to overcome.

Walt Disney

THE OFFICE

The brain is a wonderful organ; it starts working the moment you get up in the morning and does not stop until you get to the office.

Robert Frost

If your desk isn't cluttered, you probably aren't doing your job.

Harold Geneen

Most of my meetings are held in bars, and most of my phone work gets done in the car. When people ask me why

I don't even have an office, I tell them it's really very simple:
I can't sell beer to a desk.

James Koch

OPENNESS

Being open to criticism usually pays unexpected
dividends.

Harold Geneen

OPPORTUNITY

Crises, reversals, obstacles — these are always
encountered by all upper-management employees during
their careers. The value of a man under such
circumstances is not dependent only on the way in which
he confronts adversity, but also in his ability to turn
adversity to his own advantage.

John Paul Getty

Good opportunities are often disguised as hard labour.
That's why so few people recognize them.

Ann Landers

The best companies recognize that discovering
opportunities is an unpredictable process that relies a lot
on chance, and certainly not an element that can be
included in planning.

David Packard

In my opinion, modern business has a great need for more
entrepreneurs. I believe there is more opportunity for a

young man today than ever before, if only because specimens of the breed are fewer and farther between.

John Paul Getty

Small opportunities are often the origins of great enterprises.

Demosthenes

Opportunity has the sly habit of slipping in by the back door, and often it comes disguised in the form of misfortune, or temporary defeat.

Napoleon Hill

I learned that you don't get anywhere by sitting comfortably in a chair.

Conrad Hilton

If you wait for things to happen by themselves, locked up in your ivory tower, nothing will happen. You have to be on the ball, seek out events, stir people up. To find diamonds, you have to turn over a lot of stones. If you want the lights to go on and the party to begin, you have to spend time making it happen. One day I said, 'I'm not saying I won't have my Waterloo. But if it comes, I'll win.' You have to make things work, so that history becomes your destiny.

Régine

Entrepreneurs are those who understand that there is little difference between obstacle and opportunity, and are able to turn both to their advantage. Their willingness to seize initiative sets them apart from their contemporaries. Entrepreneurs don't sit on their haunches, waiting for something to happen. They make things happen.

Victor Kiam

In every life there is a moment — an event or a realization — that changes that life irrevocably. If the change is to be a happy one, one must be able to recognize the moment and seize it without delay.

Estée Lauder

OPPOSITION
See also Competition.

The breakfast of champions is not cereal, it's the opposition.

Nick Seitz

OPTIMISM
See also Positive Thinking.

The world belongs to the optimists, pessimists are only spectators.

Francois Guizot

Returning to Chicago one fateful day in 1954, I had a contract newly signed by the McDonald brothers in my briefcase. I was a veteran, riddled with scars from the business wars, but nevertheless eager to start working. I was 52 years old, diabetic, and arthritic. In my previous campaigns, I'd lost my pancreas and the major part of my thyroid gland. But I was convinced that my best years still lay ahead of me.

Ray Kroc

ORGANIZATION

Take everything, but leave me my organization, and in two years I'll be at the top again.

Henry Ford

An organizational structure that assumes that an individual in a certain position will behave in the same way as his predecessor is ridiculous.

Fletcher Byrom

The secret of the Kennedy success in politics was not money but meticulous planning and organization.

Rose Kennedy

Early on, I had the impression that a lot of work was being done for little result, and I thought that a lot of the work could be better organized.

Henry Ford

ORIGINALITY
See also Innovation.

Originality is the art of concealing your sources.

Anonymous

OWNERSHIP

The best route to the top is to own the company.

Lewis Bookwalter Ward

P

PARTNERS

My experience with Cessini taught me never to take a partner unless it's absolutely necessary. Having a partner is almost contrary to entrepreneurial philosophy. Entrepreneurs don't look to share their responsibility or their equity with anyone.

Victor Kiam

PAST EXPERIENCE

While preparing for the future, you have to step back and think about the past; but not more than a person would take a few steps back in order to jump a ditch.

Adam Mickievicz

The really progressive individuals are those who base their points of view on a profound respect of the past.

Ernest Renan

PASSION
See also Ardour; Desire.

Only passion, great passion can elevate the human soul to achieve great things.

Denis Diderot

You have to hold on to time . . . It passes all too quickly, alas. You have to hold on to it, prevent it from passing! And there is only one way to do that; to find everything interesting, to be interested in everything.

Sacha Guitry

Nothing great is ever accomplished in the world without passion.

Friedrich Hegel

PATH

I stick straight to my path, even when it bores me. I am its slave because it was I who freely chose it.

Coco Chanel

PATIENCE

Impatient people always get there too late.

Jean Dutourd

Business is like fishing: you have to have patience.

Leopold D. Silberstein

PERFECTION
See also Errors; Excellence.

Whatever deserves doing, deserves doing well.

Nicolas Poussin

I learned early that being a perfectionist and providing quality was the only way to do business.

Estée Lauder

The maxim, 'Nothing prevails but perfection' may be spelled, p-a-r-a-l-y-s-i-s.

Winston Churchill

It is better to aim for perfection and miss the target than to aim for imperfection and achieve it.

Thomas J. Watson Sr

I am what you would call a stern taskmaster. I expect perfection. And then a little more perfection when perfection is offered.

Estée Lauder

PERFORMANCE

A marathon runner is someone who can run 26 miles, 385 yards in a given amount of time, whether the standard is two-and-a-half, three, or three-and-a-half hours. But what about the fellow who runs it in ten hours? He's not a marathon runner, he's a guy wearing short pants and a pair of running shoes who is out getting some fresh air. We are defining the runner in terms of his performance. So do we define a corporate manager.

Harold Geneen

PERSEVERANCE
See also Determination; Jumping In.

Fortune is like the market where, if you stay a little, the prices will fall.

Francis Bacon

Sometimes it appears that there is a hidden Guide whose duty is to test men throughout all kinds of discouraging experiences. Those who pick themselves up after defeat and keep on trying succeed, and the world cries 'Bravo! I knew you could do it!' The hidden Guide lets no one enjoy great achievement without passing the perseverance test. Those who can't take it simply do not make the grade.

Napoleon Hill

I succeeded in business not because I was more gifted than others who failed from the start, but because I applied myself more, and I kept on applying myself for a longer time.

J.B. Duke

If I had known that it would take 40 versions before getting results, I might have given up, but luckily you always work on the principle that the next model will be the right one.

Howard Head

Nothing in the world can replace perseverance. Even talent; there's nothing more common than wasted talent. Or genius; the proverb says that geniuses are rarely rewarded. Or instruction; the world is full of educated bums. Only persistence and determination are omnipotent.

Ray Kroc

The rewards in life only come at the end of the race, not at the beginning; and you never know how long it will take to attain your goal. You might fail a thousand times, and still success is there, hidden behind the next turn in the road! You never know how close you are if you don't round that turn. I always go one step farther. If that doesn't work,

I take another step, then another. And really, one step at a time is not very difficult. I persevere until I succeed.

Og Mandino

When I got no answer and a few more months had gone by, I wrote again and said I'd love to drop by and see him again. More time passed, and I wrote another letter, suggesting a whole new way to make the deal. I was relentless, even in the face of a total lack of encouragement, because much more often than you'd think, sheer persistence is the difference between success and failure.

Donald Trump

What makes a successful businesswoman? Is it talent? Well, perhaps, although I've known many enormously successful people who were not gifted in any outstanding way, not blessed with particular talent. Is it, then, intelligence? Certainly, intelligence helps, but it's not necessarily education or the kind of intellectual reasoning needed to graduate from the Wharton School of Business that are essential. What, then, is the mystical ingredient? It's persistence. It's that certain little spirit that compels you to continue just when you're at your most tired. It's that quality that forces you to persevere, find the route around the stone wall. It's the immovable stubbornness that will not allow you to cave in when everyone says give up.

Estée Lauder

It takes twenty years to make an overnight success.

Eddie Cantor

PERSONALITY
See also Leadership.

No creative organization, research laboratory, magazine, four-star kitchen or advertising agency ever produced anything great unless it was directed by an exceptional personality.

David Ogilvy

PERSONNEL
See also Employees; Human Relations.

I am not dealing with companies, I am dealing with people.

Leopold D. Silberstein

Whether you're talking about general directors or specialists — such as buyers, production managers or sales managers — the key to all direction in business lies in directing human activities.

John Paul Getty

Any company philosophy that does not consider its human resources as its most important asset is doomed sooner or later to certain failure.

Bernard Tapie

A company is only as good as its people.

Mary Kay Ash

I discovered very quickly that in Western countries, employers would get rid of some personnel when a recession seemed imminent. It was a shock to me, because in Japan we never do this, unless we are completely desperate. If the administration takes the risk and responsibility of hiring personnel, then it also assumes responsibility for giving them work. It's not the employee who is responsible in this agreement. Also, when there is a recession, why should the personnel suffer because of a decision made by the administration who gave them a job? That's my point of view. That's why, in periods of prosperity, we increase the number of our employees with great prudence. Once hired, we try to make them understand our idea of 'shared destiny' and our intention, if the business has to deal with a recession, to give up certain benefits so that they stay with us.

Akio Morita

PERSUASION

Would you persuade, speak of interest, not of reason.

Benjamin Franklin

PHILANTHROPY
See also Charity.

The man who dies rich dies in disgrace.

Andrew Carnegie

PLANNING

Men don't plan to fail — they fail to plan.

William J. Siegel

We were spending so much time planning for the next year and the next five years that our units were not making their current quarterly earnings.

Harold Geneen

POSITIVE THINKING
See also Obstacles; Optimism.

The individual who is able to perceive a glimmer of possibility in a situation that seems, at first glance, full of insurmountable obstacles, is the one who is most likely to reap the greatest benefits.

John Paul Getty

I was a farmhand, a merchant, a clerk, a boss, a theater director and a bank director; I lived in prisons and palaces, I knew poverty and abundance, I've travelled extensively on two continents, I've met all kinds of people and seen the human character in all its guises, and time and again I have been in the greatest danger.

Amidst such a diversity of events, I had to undergo difficult times, but I'm definitely not complaining, and I believe that my life was a happy one, because I always saw the positive side of things.

P.T. Barnum

My hunger to win the game allowed me to transform every negative into a positive. No sacrifice was too great. When a snowstorm hit my region it wasn't an obstacle, it was an opportunity! The idea that my rivals would be in their homes, hiding from the elements, gave me the impetus to go from store to store, pushing my product. It was amazing how receptive a buyer could be when the snow outside his door was waist-deep and climbing, and you were the only friendly face he had seen all day.

Victor Kiam

Make the most of what you have. I operated, full time, on that precept. If you can't have everything you think you deserve at that moment, you would do well to surround yourself with symbols of your ideals. In that small office, I surrounded myself with touches of the good life, the lovely and intricately tapestried life of my imagination, an imagination that has always been, I'm proud to say, large enough to admit any possibility.

Estée Lauder

I'm not bragging, I am simply trying to show that there are always occasions where businessmen can make a good profit if they could only recognize and seize the moment, and if they could ignore the negative sentiments expressed by those who become prophets of doom.

John Paul Getty

POVERTY

Almost all great things were accomplished in poverty. Nothing is better for the creative spirit than lack of means. Luxury leads to weakness, if it doesn't kill you.

Henry David Thoreau

Poverty is attracted to the one whose mind is favourable to it, as money is attracted to him whose mind has been deliberately prepared to attract it, and through the same laws.

Napoleon Hill

I have been broke, but I have never been poor. Poverty is a state of mind. Lack of money is temporary.

Mike Todd

The major inconvenience about being poor is that it takes up all your time.

William de Kooning

Contrary to Freud, I don't think sexuality is the most important part of behaviour. Cold, hunger, and shame born of poverty are more likely to affect an individual's psychology.

Charlie Chaplin

Those who pretend that money isn't everything in life are usually broke.

Malcolm Forbes

I've been rich and I've been poor. Believe me, rich is better.

Sophie Tucker.

POWER
See also Leadership.

He who has money in his pocket has power over those who have none.

Leo Tolstoy

There is only one way to lead people, and that's to be strong, because in strength there is no error, no illusion — it is the naked truth.

Napoleon

A man who understands another is in a position to dominate him.

Baltazar Gracian

To govern people completely over a long period of time, you have to use a light hand, and not make them overly aware of their dependance.

Jean de la Bruyère

Power is the greatest aphrodisiac.

Henry Kissinger

Immense power is acquired by assuring yourself in your secret reveries that you were born to control affairs.

Andrew Carnegie

PRAISE

I believe that you should praise people whenever you can; it causes them to respond as a thirsty plant responds to water.

Mary Kay Ash

PRAYER

Work as if you were to live a hundred years. Pray as if you were to die tomorrow.

Benjamin Franklin

PREDICTIONS

In the long run, we all end up dead.

John Maynard Keynes

Prediction is very difficult, especially about the future.

Niels Bohr

It is a mistake to look too far ahead. Only one link of the chain of destiny can be handled at a time.

Winston Churchill

There are two classes of people who tell what is going to happen in the future: Those who don't know, and those who don't know they don't know.

John Kenneth Galbraith

PREPARATION
See also Planning.

Perhaps the most important thing that has come out of my life is the discovery that if you prepare yourself at every point as well as you can, with whatever means you have, however meager they may seem, you will be able to grasp opportunity for broader experience when it appears. Without preparation you cannot do it.

Eleanor Roosevelt

PRESSURE
See also Problems; Worry.

I've heard people say really often — I bet once a week — 'I wouldn't want your job for all the money in the world.' And I never respond to that. I don't know what the hell the response is. I love my job. They look upon it as a position that just grinds you down and kills you off. I don't. Maybe that's the difference. In fact, maybe that's why the guys who say things like that will never get my job.

Lee Iacocca

The best work is always carried out under pressure, and at the price of great personal effort.

William Carlos Williams

PRICE
See also Value.

Almost anything on earth can be manufactured a little less well and be sold for a little less money. And those who are only interested in prices are the main victims of this rule.

John Ruskin

Everything is worth what its purchaser will pay for it.

Publilius Syrus

The American buyer looking for a small car is so intent on saving money that he will pay any price to do so!

Lee Iacocca

PRIDE
See also Quality.

I want all our employees to think that they work in the best agency in the world. The feeling of pride produces amazing results.

David Ogilvy

I want workers to go home at night and say 'I built that car.'

Pehr G. Gyllenhammar

The pride you take in your product or service will give you the strength to deal with rejection in a positive manner.

Victor Kiam

My pride never stopped me from picking up a mop and cleaning the toilets.

Ray Kroc

I wanted to show my family and the world what I could do.

Helena Rubinstein

PRINCIPLES

When someone says to you, 'It's not a question of money, it's the principle', it's always a question of money.

Frank McKinney Hubbard

It's easy to have principles when you are rich. The important thing is to have principles when you are poor.

Ray Kroc

In business everything is subject to change — people, products, buildings, machinery, everything — except principles. To paraphrase Thomas Jefferson, in matters of principle, stand like a rock; in other matters, swim with the current. So, while I strongly advocate flexibility, when it comes to principles we must stand firm.

Mary Kay Ash

PROBLEMS
See also Pressure; Worry.

Problems are opportunities in work clothes.

Henry J. Kaiser

The weak have problems. The strong have solutions.

Louis Pauwels

A problem that is well formulated is half resolved.

Charles F. Kettering

I proceed with a courageous and honest analysis of the situation. Then I determine what the worst consequences of my failure could be. After imagining the most disastrous consequences that could result, I resign myself to accept them in case it becomes necessary. From that moment on, I consecrate all my time and energy to looking for ways that could alleviate the consequences which, mentally, I have already accepted.

Dale Carnegie

Our problems are man-made; therefore they can be solved by men. And man can be as big as he wants. No problem of human destiny is beyond human beings.

John Fitzgerald Kennedy

If anything can go wrong, it will, and at the most inopportune time.

Murphy's Law

PRODUCT

What you need more than anything to create a new product that sells is a total understanding of the tastes, wishes and needs of the consumers.

William J. McDonald

It is not the product that we sell, but rather what the product can do to solve the clients' problems.

Francis G. Rodgers

When the product is good, it does not need an ace marketing job.

Lee Iacocca

PROFIT
See also Money; Rewards.

The engine which drives Enterprise is not thrift, but profit.

John Maynard Keynes

Profitability is the sovereign criterion of the enterprise.

Peter Drucker

Business without profit is not business, any more than a pickle is not a candy.

Charles F. Abbott

What's worth doing is worth doing for money.

Joseph Donohue

General Motors is not in the business of making cars. General Motors is in the business of making money.

Thomas A. Murphy

Making profit a vice is a socialist idea. As for myself, I consider the real vice to be taking a loss.

Winston Churchill

You never lose money by making a profit.

Anonymous

Profit is only a by-product of a good operation, and not an end in itself.

Thomas Peters and Robert Waterman

If you think first in terms of your clients, all the rest falls into place, and you make a profit.

Rich Port

The boss is a salaried worker who has to invest his profits in the business every year.

Bernard Tapie

If a man goes into business with only the idea of making money, the chances are he won't.

Joyce Clyde Hall

If your cow doesn't give milk, sell it.

John Peers

PROGRESS

Technological progress is like an axe in the hands of a psychopath.

Albert Einstein

Computers are useless. They only give you answers.

Pablo Picasso

PROMOTION
See also Advancement.

Earn more for those under you and for those over you, and your rise is almost inevitable.

Michael Korda

PROPERTY

I have no sense of property. I am not interested in ownership.

Robert Maxwell

PRUDENCE
See also Realism.

Be confident, without pulling the wool over your eyes. A lot of people have remained poor, or ruined themselves, because of this destructive tendency. These people see a sure success in every undertaking, which is why they stick to nothing, abandoning one business after another. The fable about the hunter who sells the bearskin before he shoots the bear shows that this tendency goes a long way back. Unfortunately, the fable and experience have not cured people of the habit.

P.T. Barnum

The point is that you mustn't be too greedy. If you go for a home run on every pitch, you're also going to strike out a lot. I try never to leave myself too exposed, even if it means sometimes settling for a triple, a double, or even, on rare occasions, a single.

Donald Trump

It was this philosophy, that there is no bottom to the barrel — it was this philosophy that led to the 1929 stock market crash and seven of the worst years this country ever faced. It was this same philosophy that led to the construction of a miniature golf course on every corner in Los Angeles, and the horrible, tragic crash of this industry — taking with it all the little people involved.

Howard Hughes

PSYCHOLOGY

Aside from all the courses on industrial management and economy, I studied psychology and pathology for four years. I'm not kidding when I say that these courses were probably the most valuable in my entire university career; they have been more useful in dealing with all the crazies that I've had occasion to work with in the automobile business than all the courses on mechanics combined.

Lee Iacocca

PUBLIC OPINION

When, as a young and unknown man, I started to be successful, I was referred to as a gambler. My operations increased in scope and volume. Then I was known as a speculator. The sphere of my activities continued to expand, and soon I was known as a banker. Actually, I was doing the same thing all the time!

Sir Ernest Cassel

The only sin which people never forgive in each other is a difference of opinion.

Ralph Waldo Emerson

The businessman who goes against the current of popular opinion should expect to be opposed, derided and damned. That's what made me rich!

John Paul Getty

A man labelled a 'billionaire' lives well and he's very lucky to enjoy innumerable privileges and comforts — but he really can't win. If he spends freely, he's accused of being a wastrel and of trying to make an impression by splashing money around. If he lives quietly and without flashy ostentation, he's castigated for being penurious — a 'tightwad'.

John Paul Getty

PUNCTUALITY

Punctuality is the soul of business.

Thomas Haliburton

PUNISHMENT

No reasonable man punishes for a fault already committed, but to prevent faults from being committed.

Seneca

Q

QUALITY
See also Pride.

Quality — Service — Propriety — and Price: If I'd been
given a brick every time I had to repeat those words, I think
I could have built a bridge across the Atlantic Ocean!

Ray Kroc

I made the firm resolution never to join a business where
money took precedence over quality of the work, neither
from the banking or a financing point of view. I also
resolved, if I was not able to find support for an
undertaking liable to be run with the public interest at
heart, to renounce the undertaking entirely. Because my
own attempts, supported by observation of what was
going on around me, convinced me that businesses run on
the sole principle of making money were not very
interesting, and were not worthy of a serious man who
wanted to accomplish something. As for the rest, I'm still
waiting to be shown that this is not the right way to make
money. Because in my opinion, the only basis for a serious
enterprise is the high quality of its products.

Henry Ford

QUESTIONING
See also Instinct.

I like to think I have that instinct. That's why I don't hire a lot of number-crunchers, and I don't trust fancy marketing surveys. I do my own surveys and draw my own conclusions. I'm a great believer in asking everyone for an opinion before I make a decision. It's a natural reflex. If I'm thinking of buying a piece of property, I'll ask the people who live nearby about the area — what they think of the schools and the crime and the shops. When I'm in another city and I take a cab, I'll always make it a point to ask the cab-driver questions. I ask and I ask and I ask, until I begin to get a gut feeling about something. And that's when I make a decision.

Donald Trump

R

RAT RACE

You're a mouse, studying to be a rat.

Wilson Mizner

The trouble with the rat race is that even if you win you're still a rat.

Lily Tomlin

READING

Reading good books is like conversing with the most honest people of past centuries.

René Descartes

REALISM
See also Prudence.

What counts is knowing that you can't do everything, that there are obstacles which cannot always be overcome without sufficient power. You have to accept that you cannot overcome them, and admit that if you can't lift fifty pounds, you should do some exercise, and not try to lift them before you're in shape. And when you are in shape, it will be easy ...

Bernard Tapie

REASON

Two excesses: exclude reason, and accept nothing but reason.

Blaise Pascal

Nothing is ever accomplished by a reasonable man.

J. Fred Bucy

The best person's reasons are always the strongest.

Victor Hugo

RECESSION

It seems like the only thing that we can count on in the United States is that even during the hardest of recessions, the rich get richer.

Lee Iacocca

RELIGION
See also God.

God exists in details.

Robert Goizueta

I believe in God, in the family, and in McDonald's. And at the office that order is reversed.

Ray Kroc

In His great charity, the Lord does not allow us to see the future, because if we did we might wish to put an end to our lives.

Lee Iacocca

As soon as you use the word 'God' with understanding, belief and knowledge, you establish the highest vibration known to man. This vibratory influence assembles substantive material, and when you express your thoughts, the material belongs to you.

Baird T. Spalding

REPRIMAND

Condemn the fault, and not the actor of it!

William Shakespeare

If you humiliate people publicly, they may support you publicly, but they will hate you privately.

Vernon Walters

REPUTATION

There is only one thing in the world worse than being talked about, and that is not being talked about.

Oscar Wilde

RESPONSIBILITY

I believe that the social responsibility of today's corporations is fundamentally the same as it always has been: to earn profits for shareholders by serving consumer needs with maximum efficiency. This is not the whole of the matter, but it is the heart of the matter.

Henry Ford II

I am responsible for everything, therefore everything must be perfect.

Régine

RESULTS

Don't talk to me about your efforts. Talk to me about your results.

James Ling

In business, the big salaries go to those who produce results. That goes for the directors, as well as for those who are dependent on the directors' results.

J.C. Aspley

RETIREMENT

Being tempted to rest and enjoy the fruits of your labour is only natural. I understand perfectly well that a person would like to exchange a life of labour for a life of rest. I've had the desire myself. But I believe that when a person wants to rest, he should retire completely from the business world. And that's not in my future plans. I consider my success as incitement to do better.

Henry Ford

In every enterprise, consider where you will end up.

Publilius Syrus

I believe that you have to plan your retirement, not by thinking that you will be deprived of something, but rather that something will be added to your life. You see, you do not start from zero, you are rich with the totality of experience that life has given to you. The past years are like a crown which you wear at the beginning of the next phase of your life.

Colonel Sanders

I declare war on the word retire. Look at the dictionary: retreat of an army after a lost combat.

Marcel Blenstein-Blanchet

I must state that high-level executives are not subject to forced retirement; a number of them continue to fulfil their functions right up to the age of 70 or 75.

Akio Morita

Let's face facts: retirement is a horrible obligation. I have always found it ridiculous that a person is forced to retire at the age of 65, even if he is in full possession of his faculties. We should continue to have confidence in older management, because they have the experience and the wisdom. In Japan, the older executives are at the helm. On my last visit to the land of the rising sun, my youngest colleague was 65 years old! And you can't say that Japanese industry is faring badly!

Lee Iacocca

REWARDS
See also Profit.

I don't deserve this award, but I have arthritis and I don't deserve that either.

Jack Benny

Make money and the whole world will call you Sir.

Mark Twain

My idea was then and still is that if a man did his work well, the price he could get for that work, the profits, and all financial matters would care for themselves.

Henry Ford

The journey is the reward.

Steven Jobs

RICHES
See also Money.

I want money, just so I can be rich.

John Lennon

Riches are irritating. You always have to excuse yourself when you have money.

Lilianne Bettencourt

I don't know exactly how much I possess, except what is in my pocket.

Marcel Blenstein-Blanchet

Fortune does not change except for those who do not know how to conform to the times.

Machiavelli

Always keep the thought of the riches of God in your mind. If another thought interferes, replace it, and bless this abundance. If necessary, give constant thanks for the works of God. Be content to bless and be thankful for the fulfilling of His work, for the working of God in you, and for the fulfilment of your desires, because all you want is to spread goodness around you.

Baird T. Spalding

RIDICULE

Ridicule does not exist: those who dare confront it head on will conquer the world.

Octave Mirabeau

THE RIGHT PERSON FOR THE JOB

I have always believed that success would be the inevitable result . . .if we sent the right person to fill the right place.

Austen Henry Layard

The most important man in the room is the one who knows what to do next.

James L. Webb

RISK

There are a thousand men who want security for every one man who is willing to take risks.

John Paul Getty

There is absolutely nothing special about walking on a rope stretched along the ground. Where there is no risk, there can be no pride in a deed accomplished, and therefore no happiness.

Ray Kroc

Every time I took a risk, I made sure that the research and marketing reports were favourable to my instincts.

Lee Iacocca

Winning without danger means triumph without glory.

Pierre Corneille

Entrepreneurs are risk-takers, willing to roll the dice with their money or reputations on the line in support of an idea or enterprise. They willingly assume responsibility for the success or failure of a venture and are answerable for all its facets. The buck not only stops at their desks, it starts there, too.

Victor Kiam

Risk is the absolute driving force behind innovation. When you have a new idea, how do you expect people to react? Original ideas are systematically rejected by everyone, and it takes time for today's utopias to become tomorrow's realities. Aragon wrote: 'real geniuses provide the ideas for twenty years later.'

Bernard Tapie

It's essential to take a minimum of risk. But I am aware that this does not concern everyone. There are some people who cannot leave home in the morning without an umbrella, even if the sun is shining.

Lee Iacocca

I'd risk the rent, but if it worked, I would start the business I always dreamed about. Risk-taking is the cornerstone of empires.

Estée Lauder

ROLE MODELS

What I retained most about this man [Napoleon] was a kind of moral philosophy which guided all his future orientation; that of the little student from a poor family, who was able to scoff at kings, proclaim a revolution and dominate the entire Western world. And I too, one day, would be like Napoleon, small and famous. Napoleon, my dear Napoleon, the model for all my childish ambitions, since we all have the right to our crazy dreams.

Soichiro Honda

S

SALARY

If you pay peanuts, you get monkeys.

Anonymous

SAVINGS

Whatever you have, spend less.

Samuel Johnson

Economy: cutting down other people's wages.

J.B. Morton

Money is made to be spent. But that doesn't mean you have to throw it out the window. Because I could come up with millions for my friends, or to promote my artists, but I still finish the last piece of bread on my plate, and I always close the light when I leave the room.

Eddie Barclay

I never threw money around. I learned from my father that every penny counts, because before too long your pennies turn into dollars. To this day, if I feel a contractor is overcharging me, I'll pick up the phone, even if it's only for $5,000 or $10,000, and I'll complain. People say to me, 'What are you bothering for, over a few bucks?' My answer is that the day I can't pick up the telephone and make a twenty-five cent call to save $10,000 is the day I'm going to close up shop.

Donald Trump

[When asked why he eliminated first-class air travel for members of the firm]: The front of the plane arrives at the same time as the rear.

Victor Kiam

Small change makes large sums.

Helena Rubinstein

SCHOOL
See also Diplomas; Education.

At school, if you pass the exam and get twenty out of twenty, that's perfect. But if you forget one word on your paper, you get zero. In the business world, you have exams every day. You don't get a twenty, but millions of points, or sometimes only ten. But if you make a mistake, it's not a zero you get. A mistake always means a minus something.

Akio Morita

SECRETS

I have ways of making money you know nothing about.

John Rockefeller

Let a man start out in life to build something better and sell it cheaper than it has been built or sold before, let him have that determination and the money will roll in.

Henry Ford

Ideas and men; these are the two key words of business. Because of what value is a good idea without the men to make it real?

Bernard Tapie

There is no secret ingredient, no cabalistic formula that can explain the success of the most prosperous Japanese companies. No theory, no plan, no system of government can assure the success of an enterprise. Only people can do that. The most important task of a Japanese company leader — any company — is to establish sane relations with the personnel, to give them the feeling of belonging to a family in which each member, worker or executive, has a common interest in the future.

Akio Morita

SEDUCTION
See also Ambition.

And very quickly we had to fight, make money, and this way of making money through selling, which means seducing by capturing people's attention through words, gestures, sighs and charm, is something, I must admit, that aroused a profound sense of joy in me, which I have never lost.

Bernard Tapie

SEEDS
See also Beginnings.

All flowers of the future are the seeds of today.

Chinese Proverb

I drop this nut in this bowl of water. Where it hits the water there forms the center of a series of concentric waves. The waves grow until they reach the edge of the bowl. To the eye, they seem to lose their force and stop. In reality, when they reach the limit of the bowl they turn back toward the center. This is the exact representation of all our thoughts and words. Thoughts and words create certain vibrations, which spread out to the limits of the universe. Then they return to their point of origin. All our thoughts and words, good or bad, come back to us as surely as they were created.

Baird T. Spalding

SELF-KNOWLEDGE

It usually happens that people hold us in the same esteem we hold ourselves.

Marquis de Vauvenargues

No one can make you feel small without your consent.

Eleanor Roosevelt

The first rule comes from Socrates who said, 'Know thyself.' That's the first commandment of any boss worth the title today. You have to know yourself with enough humility to appreciate your areas of deficiency, so that you can apply the fundamental rule of complementary competence, since a boss is nothing if he's not surrounded by associates, both young and old, lucid and pessimistic, delirious and wise.

Bernard Tapie

Real greatness consists of being master of yourself.

Daniel Defoe

SELLING
See also Buying.

In the modern business world, being an original and creative brain is useless if you are not able to sell what you create. Don't expect the management of a company to recognize a good idea if it is not presented to them by a good sales person.

David Ogilvy

Everyone lives by selling something.

Robert Louis Stevenson

Any fool can paint a picture, but it takes a wise man to be able to sell it.

Samuel Butler

When you are seated in front of someone important, imagine that person wearing longjohns. That's how I always proceed in business.

Joseph Kennedy

I always look each person squarely in the eyes and, whenever possible, try to say something personal. It might be only a comment such as 'I love your hair,' or 'What a beautiful dress you're wearing,' but I give each person my undivided attention, and I don't allow anything to distract me. Each person whose hand I shake is the most important person in the world to me at that moment.

Mary Kay Ash

The merchant's art consists of taking an article from where it is plentiful, and bringing it somewhere that it is rare.

Ralph Waldo Emerson

You have to sell yourself.

Joe Girard

Production minus sales equals zero.

Shelby H. Carter Jr

The average salesperson spends less than 25 per cent of their time face-to-face with their clients. Personally, I spend 90 per cent. That's the only way to make money in sales.

Edna Larsen

In the factory, we manufacture cosmetics. In the store, we sell hopes.

Charles Revlon

There is no such thing as 'soft sell' or 'hard sell.' There is only 'smart sell' and 'stupid sell.'

Charles Brower

The average sale is made after the prospect has said 'no' six times.

Jeffrey P. Davidson

Most salesmen try to take the horse to water and make him drink. Your job is to make the horse thirsty.

Gabriel M. Siegel

You can't sell anything that you wouldn't buy yourself.

Victor Kiam

You have to try to tell people what they want to hear, but without ever lying to them. Make them laugh, tell them stories — it's up to you how you do it. But under no circumstances forget that you have at most five minutes to convince them and prove your case, ten minutes at best. Each second counts, and the least error is fatal. That's when I came up with the 'three twenties' formula: the first twenty words, the first twenty seconds, and the twenty centimeters of your face.

Bernard Tapie

Don't forget that the people you're selling to are as egotistical as you are. They don't care a hoot about you or your interests or what would benefit you. What they're looking for is service.

Akio Morita

SERIOUSNESS
See also Pressure.

One of the symptoms of an approaching nervous breakdown is the belief that one's work is terribly important.

Bertrand Russell

I often ruminate over ideas in the car, which is why my associates insist I have a chauffeur. They were afraid that I'd have an accident, because I was thinking too hard. So they thought it was better for me — and for Wang Laboratories — if I didn't drive. In general, I don't like the image and ostentation associated with the president of a corporation. I only own two suits at a time, and I replace them when they're worn out.

An Wang

Sometimes — not often, but sometimes — less is more.

Donald Trump

If a Japanese client is called to the office of a new company and finds luxurious surroundings, spacious private offices etc. he asks himself if this company is serious, since it spent so much money on its own appearance and not enough on the products it manufactures.

Akio Morita

SERVICE

For me, money is not everything. As I have already said, I was more interested in doing good and helping people. It's like the Rotary Club slogan that induced me to become a member more than 50 years ago: 'Service first.'

Colonel Sanders

The greatest among you are those who serve others.

Baird T. Spalding

SEX

Those who succeed the most are people with a highly developed sexuality, who have learned to transform their sexual energy.

Napoleon Hill

within every man's ability to transform some of his sex
otion into a dynamic drive which brings success.

Napoleon Hill

SIESTA
See also Sleep.

I found I could add nearly two hours to my working day
by going to bed for an hour after luncheon.

Winston Churchill

SIMPLICITY

The key to quality is in the simplicity of production. 'I have
a great idea.' How many times have I heard this refrain?
And I always say to myself, 'Yeah, so great that it's
impossible to do.'

Lee Iacocca

KISS: Keep It Simple, Stupid.

Anonymous

Well you can only wear one pair of shoes at a time!

Ray Kroc

SINGLE-MINDEDNESS
See also Obsession.

To make an idea succeed, you have to concentrate on that
idea alone. Or if you prefer: To succeed you must only have
one idea in mind.

André Gide

SIXTH SENSE

Comparatively speaking, Japanese business leaders seem to possess a kind of Oriental sixth sense. Instead of juxtaposing facts, they look at an idea from a holistic point of view, and relay this information to their sixth sense in order to decide on a course of action. So they have a better grasp of the situation than someone who sees it only in parts.

Akio Morita

SIZE

The dinosaur's eloquent lesson is that if some bigness is good, an overabundance of bigness is not necessarily better.

Eric Johnston

SLEEP

My secret resides in the fact that I fully exploit each minute of rest. I don't think I sleep more than six hours a night on the average. I've often made do with four or less, and I'm convinced that if I hadn't used the technique of self-hypnosis I couldn't have made it through many a day. What's more, I hate being inactive, even for a minute. I was determined to live in comfort, which I can now afford thanks to the revenues from my two jobs.

Ray Kroc

SMILING

If they are not sold in ten minutes after they are cooked, Big Macs have to be thrown out. For fries, say seven minutes. And the cashiers have to greet each customer with a smile.

Ray Kroc

You should not trust someone who never smiles.

Henri de Montherlant

When, in your daily life, you meet someone too weak to smile, give him yours. Because no one needs a smile more than the person who can't smile himself.

Dale Carnegie

SOLITUDE

Nothing can be accomplished without solitude.

Pablo Picasso

SPEAKING

Speak to people about themselves, and they'll listen for hours.

Benjamin Disraeli

Never tell someone they're wrong: that's a disastrous tactic.

Dale Carnegie

To judge how much we bother people when we speak about ourselves, we have to consider how much we are bothered when others talk about themselves.

Madame de Sévigné

I often tell a story about the first time I gave a speech. I was so nervous that I kept my eyes closed throughout most of the monologue. I kept hoping that if I didn't look at them they would quietly go away. When I had finished, I opened my eyes and discovered that, unfortunately, my wish had been granted. There was only one person left in the audience. He was a bookish-looking fellow wearing a sour expression. Hoping to find some solace in this catastrophe, I asked him why he stayed. Still frowning, he replied, 'I'm the next speaker.'

Victor Kiam

SPECIALITY

Make sure that everyone is doing the work they know best.

Aristophanes

May each person exercise the art he know best.

Cicero

The person who possesses a perfect understanding of his work, plus the ability to influence his colleagues, will rise higher than the rest. That person will attain success.

Dale Carnegie

SPECULATION

Practically no one has retained a fortune based on speculation.

Andrew Carnegie

There are two moments in a man's life when he should not speculate: when he doesn't have the means, and when he does have the means.

Mark Twain

SPENDING
See also Money.

The current misconception is that money can solve all your problems. Money creates problems, and the more you have the greater are your problems. And one of the biggest problems is knowing how to spend it wisely.

Ray Kroc

Spending increases in order to meet revenues.

C. Northcote Parkinson

Prosperity (and I'm mainly talking about sudden prosperity) is a more difficult test for people than adversity. It is unfortunately too common to see people who acquire sudden wealth to start spending wildly and to eat away their revenue and capital in a short time. Ruin is the only thing you win in this kind of ridiculous game of wanting to impress people and have them talk about you.

P.T. Barnum

STARS
See also Destiny.

You have to believe in your star before believing in galaxies. There should be a complete symbiosis between your profile and your path. There is no great destiny until you have chosen the cause you are going to fight for, whether your choice was based on opportunism or calculation.

Bernard Tapie

STATE OF MIND
See also Confidence; Mind.

As soon as you become rich, you realize that you really didn't need to work all that hard, that it was your state of mind as well as having a precisely defined goal that were most important to achieving your success.

Napoleon Hill

STATISTICS

There are three kinds of lies: lies, damned lies and statistics.

Benjamin Disraeli

STOCK EXCHANGE

There are only two emotions on Wall Street: fear and greed.

William M. LeFevre Jr

There is absolutely no moral difference between someone who plays cards, lotteries or horse races, and someone who plays the stock exchange. The approach is just as perverse.

Theodore Roosevelt

October is one of the worst months to play the stock exchange. Other bad months are: July, January, September, April, November, May, March, June, December, August and February.

Mark Twain

I buy when others sell.

John Paul Getty

STRATEGY
See also Negotiation.

A good archer hits the target even before shooting.

Tch'ao Pou-Tché

Carefully prepare your strategy, then strike like lightning: that is the great and simple secret of men of action. If there are few of them, it is because patience and decision are rarely found in the same person.

Jacques de Bourbon Busset

The worst thing you can possibly do in a deal is seem desperate to make it. That makes the other guy smell blood, and then you're dead. The best thing you can do is deal from strength, and leverage is the biggest strength you can have. Leverage is having something the other guy wants. Or better yet, needs. Or best of all, simply can't do without.

Donald Trump

STRESS
See also Pressure.

Nature likes variety. Remember this, not only in planning your day, but in planning your life. Our civilization tends to force people into highly specialized occupations which may become monotonously repetitive. Remember that stress is the great equalizer of biologic activities and if you use the same parts of your body or mind over and over again, the only means Nature has to force you out of the groove is general (systemic) stress.

Hans Selye

You have to stand on the promontory against which the waves are incessantly breaking. The promontory remains standing, while all around the waves crash. 'I'm so unlucky that something like that could happen to me.' But no, on the contrary: 'I'm so lucky that it happened, I will not succumb to anxiety, I will not be broken nor frightened by the future.' This kind of thing could happen to anyone, but not anyone could overcome it and remain free of discouragement.

Marcus Aurelius

STRUGGLE

See also Adversity; Crisis; Defeat; Effort; Elbow Grease; Extra Mile; Failure.

The right way to live is to struggle so that you never die.

Guy de Rothschild

STUPIDITY

Many present day managers — holding MBAs or the equivalent — are perhaps a little too intelligent. They're the ones who change direction all the time, who come up with a hundred variations of a plan, who conceive of complicated systems, who concoct graphs and statistic sheets. They're the ones with 200-page strategic plans, and 500-page documents which analyse market requirements that only represent one stage of the product's development.

Our 'super idiot' friends are different. They don't understand why all products cannot be of the best quality. They don't understand why each client cannot get the very best personalized service, even when dealing with chips. They take a defective bottle as a personal affront. They don't understand why it's impossible to have a continuous flow of new products, or why a worker cannot make a suggestion every fifteen days. They are really simple-minded — simpletons really. Yes, simple can have a negative connotation, but the directors of the best companies really are a bit simple.

Thomas Peters and Robert Waterman

Be stupid, foolish, naïve and lazy. Be stupid enough to think that what you desire is possible. Be foolish enough to devote all your energy to it. Foolish enough not to stop when people throw stones at you (a moving target is harder to hit!). Be naïve enough to understand that you can't do it all yourself, and share the adventure with others. Be lazy enough to find someone to do the work for you. You have to take time out to think.

Meshulam Riklis

SUBSERVIENCE

I handed in my resignation, resolved never to accept another subservient position. It's certainly easier only to work during office hours, to do your job during the day and leave it behind at night and not think about it until the next day, and you can get along very well like this if you have the type of character that is content to be ordered around, to be a faithful employee perhaps, but never a director or a boss.

Henry Ford

SUBSIDY

When an enterprise ceases to be an investment and becomes a subsidy, you should have the courage to drop it.

Sir James Goldsmith

SUCCESS
See also Getting Ahead.

A man has succeeded when he wakes up in the morning, goes to bed at night, and does what he likes between the two.

Bob Dylan

The success of one person depends on the success of others.

John Rockefeller

Nothing succeeds like success.

English proverb

If you want to succeed, you have to forge new paths and avoid borrowed ones.

John Rockefeller

Anyone who has attained success is regularly asked the same question by people he or she meets: 'How can I, or anyone else, do it too?' When I tell them how I started out creating the base for my own business, as a drilling operator four decades ago, they usually reply: 'But you were lucky, you started your business at a time when it was still possible to make millions, you couldn't do it again today. Nobody could.'

I cannot help but be perplexed by this negative, and I think erroneous attitude, proffered by otherwise intelligent people. Assuredly, there exists a mass of facts which prove that young, dynamic, imaginative and hustling people have more opportunity to attain wealth and success today than ever before in our history. Innumerable young businessmen, aware and aggressive, have shown this to be true over the last few years by making a fortune in a variety of ways.

John Paul Getty

To succeed, all you have to do is talk about yourself 80 per cent of the time.

Woody Allen

The first suggestion consists of placing the idea and the word 'God' in the mind, and of positively knowing that all success stems from Him. Then adjust this idea of success with the thought 'God, I Am Success.' Then comes the following thought: 'God, I am completely capable of succeeding in any effort that I sincerely undertake.' And then the following affirmation: 'God, I am that precise knowledge that accompanies the ability to succeed.' And next: 'God, I am that infinite love which will attract all those elements essential to my success.'

Baird T. Spalding

Most people know what ingredients are necessary for success. The only problem is that they are not ready to pay the price.

Rich Port

Success is the result of unrelenting labour.

Paul Ricard

Nothing is more capricious than success, for us and for you. Don't let it get away.

Ray Kroc

Success is due to about 15 per cent technological know-how and 85 per cent personality.

Dale Carnegie

Success didn't spoil me, I've always been insufferable.

Fran Lebowitz

The art of being very audacious and very careful at the same time is the art of success.

Napoleon

I am always astonished to see so many talented people fall in one way or another during their lives. People fail to achieve what they planned to do, or if they do achieve something, alas, they are too often shot down by the outrageous slings of bad fortune. Despite the fact that luck certainly plays a role in success or failure, I am convinced that there are no secrets for success. People usually fail because of their own mistakes. If someone seems to progress without error, others ascribe it to some kind of genius. Success depends more on common sense than on genius.

An Wang

If a guy has a really good success pattern, I'll go along with him if he says he can go to the moon on Scotch tape.

Raymond Herzog

SUCCESSOR

In my opinion, a man of quality should tell his father to stuff his money and build something on his own.

Bernard Tapie

As soon as you have started your company, train a relative, a friend, or a member of your staff whom you trust, and who could replace you in case of illness.

Ron Hoglend

SUPERIORITY

Being superior to others has never required great effort. What is difficult is the desire to be superior to yourself.

Claude Debussy

SURE THING

You could say that the only sure thing is that in business there are no sure things.

Akio Morita

T

TAKEOVER

It is better to take over and build upon an existing business than to start a new one.

Harold Geneen

I liked it so much, I bought the company!

Victor Kiam

TALENT
See also Genius.

Don't misunderstand me. I'm in no way saying that we are born businessmen instead of becoming businessmen. I would be the last person in the world to propose such a theory, because my own example and my experience indicate that the contrary is probably true. From all the evidence, I was in no way a born businessman.

John Paul Getty

TAXES

There is nothing that a government learns faster than how to get money from its citizens.

Adam Smith

Income tax has made more Americans into liars than golf. Even when you fill out your tax forms with the best intentions in the world, you never know in the end whether you are a swindler or a martyr.

Will Rogers

The most difficult thing in the world to understand is taxes.

Albert Einstein

We owe the invention of progressive taxation to Karl Marx.

Ronald Reagan

There's only one way to get out of paying taxes, and that is to make a fortune.

Pierre Samuel Du Pont de Nemours

TAXPAYERS

The taxpayer — a person who works for the administration without passing the entrance exam.

Ronald Reagan

TEAMWORK

All commercial operations can, in the final analysis, be summed up in three words: personnel, products, profits. Personnel comes first. Without a good team, it is impossible to expect anything from the other two.

Lee Iacocca

My second principle is the necessity to create team spirit amongst personnel. I got the employees together and told them that their behaviour would help make the clients happy so they'd come back. I applied this formula my whole life long.

Conrad Hilton

TELEPHONES

There is no typical week in my life. I wake up most mornings very early, around six, and spend the first hour or so of each day reading the morning newspapers. I usually arrive at my office by nine, and I get on the phone.

Donald Trump

At home, I have five telephone lines, two of which are for my personal use. I also have special lines in our Hawaii apartment, in the Museum Tower in New York, and in our country house at Lake Ashi, near Fuji Yama.

Akio Morita

THEORY

You cannot run a business, or anything else, on a theory.

Harold Geneen

THINKING

The real problem is not whether machines think, but whether men do.

B.F. Skinner

When you begin to think and grow rich you will observe that riches begin with a state of mind, with definiteness of purpose, with little or no hard work.

Napoleon Hill

You should act as a thinking man, and think as a man of action.

Henri Bergson

While we stop to think, we often miss an opportunity.

Publilius Syrus

Wealth is the product of man's capacity to think.

Ayn Rand

Most people would sooner die than think; in fact they do so.

Bertrand Russell

No one is subject to more faults than the person who acts only upon reflection.

Marquis de Vauvenargues

THINKING BIG
See also Ambition.

I like thinking big. I always have. To me it's very simple: if you're going to be thinking anyway, you might as well think big. Most people think small, because most people are afraid of success, afraid of making decisions, afraid of winning. And that gives people like me a great advantage.

Donald Trump

I was convinced that if you think small, you stay small, and I had no intention of staying small!

Ray Kroc

One hundred cars a day, that's the minimum, and I soon hope to multiply this figure by ten. If I had followed the advice of my associates, I would have been content to maintain my business at it's present level, and to use the money to build a nice administration building, and from time to time produce a new model to stimulate the public's interest. In other words, to become a peaceful and serious businessman. But I thought farther, much farther, and much bigger than that.

Henry Ford

To my mind, the world is just too small. I don't need a university degree. One day what I do will astonish you!

Aristotle Onassis

I will become the Napoleon of mechanics!

Soichiro Honda

People will discover that I had an amazing imagination, and that my plans were enormous.

Régine

TIME

Hurry up and start living well, with the thought that each day is a life unto itself.

Seneca

Each person's time is fixed: but for everyone, the time in life is brief. Prolonging your renown through your actions is the result of valour.

Virgil

We do not merit glory until we know the value of time.

Marquis de Vauvenargues

Work expands so as to fill the time available for its completion. General recognition of this fact is shown in the proverbial phrase, 'It is the busiest man who has time to spare.'

C. Northcote Parkinson

Dost thou love life? Then do not squander Time, for that is the stuff life is made of.

Benjamin Franklin

To choose time is to save time.

Francis Bacon

The less one has to do, the less time one finds to do it in.

Lord Chesterfield

In parting, I would remind you that 'Life is a checkerboard, and the player opposite you is Time. If you hesitate before moving, or neglect to move promptly, your men will be wiped off the board by time. You are playing against a partner who will not tolerate indecision!'

Napoleon Hill

Everything comes to the man who hurries while waiting.

Thomas A. Edison

The worst and most costly kind of waste is of time, because it is invisible.

Thomas Bata

We can't have a crisis next week. My agenda is already full.

Henry Kissinger

A very busy man rarely changes his mind.

Friedrich Nietzsche

Lost time cannot be recovered.

Benjamin Franklin

There is never enough time, unless you use it.

Malcolm Forbes

Shaking hands is a waste of time.

Robert Hersant

He that will not apply new remedies must expect new evils: for time is the greatest innovator.

Francis Bacon

I live today as if it were my last. And what would I do with this precious day that remains? Most importantly, I would seal the container so that not one drop of life falls into the sand. I would not waste a single moment of this day complaining about yesterday's problems, or yesterday's setbacks and torments, because good always comes from bad, doesn't it?

Can you put the sand back in a broken hourglass? Can the sun rise where it set? Can I erase yesterday's mistakes, or correct them? Can I be younger than yesterday? Can I take back the bad words that were spoken, the blows that were struck, the suffering that was inflicted? No! Yesterday is dead and buried forever, and I will not think about it ever again. I will live this day as if it were my last.

Og Mandino

The good old days are here and now.

Denis Waitley

Carpe Diem! [Seize the day!]

Horace

Can anybody remember when the times were not difficult and money not scarce?

Ralph Waldo Emerson

My guiding principle has been to avoid putting things off for tomorrow.

Duke of Wellington

Parkinson's Law of Triviality: The time spent on any item of the agenda will be in inverse proportion to the sum involved.

C. Northcote Parkinson

Work expands so as to fill the time available for its completion ... The thing to be done swells in importance and complexity in a direct ratio with the time to be spent.

C. Northcote Parkinson

Nine-tenths of wisdom is being wise in time.

Theodore Roosevelt

Forget watching the clock. Nine-to-five doesn't exist for you. Business is a game, and eight hours doesn't afford you enough innings to score the deciding run. When I first hit the road as a salesman I noticed that none of my rivals worked weekends. I had nothing particularly important to do on Saturdays; I was single at the time and was unencumbered by the responsibilities of marriage. What was I going to do — play tennis? Selling was my game, and I intended to be a winner.

Victor Kiam

The ability to concentrate and make optimum use of time is vital for anyone who wants to succeed in business, as well as in almost any other field. Aside from crisis periods, I never worked on Friday night, Saturday or Sunday.

Lee Iacocca

Like Balzac, who considered a night of love as the sacrifice of a page of a novel, I also considered it as the sacrifice of a good day's work in the studio.

Charlie Chaplin

TIMING

He who comes late to the table finds nothing but bones.

Latin Proverb

It is not enough to be a great man, you have to be in the right place at the right time.

Georges Pompidou

TITLES

This title of Colonel before my name is like the honourable Sir in front of yours, my dear Sir Lawyer. It means absolutely nothing.

Colonel Sanders

TOUGH

The time to be toughest is when things are going the best.

Donald E. Keoch

TOYS

The difference between a man and a child is the price of his toys.

Malcolm Forbes

TRAINING
See also Education.

Education knows no saturation point.

Thomas J. Watson Sr

Business schools do not prepare you to run a large company.

Reginald H. Jones

Schools of management, more than any other single element, have assured the success of the Japanese and German invasion of the American market.

M. Edward Wrapp

True education consists of learning from the best parts of yourself.

Mahatma Gandhi

TRAVEL

I stopped counting my voyages across the Pacific long ago, but not because it's as tiring as you may think. You see, in a plane I sleep marvellously well. I just have to wrap myself in a blanket, and I rest better than in any hotel room. People ask for my secret. Well, I carry a box of sushi with me — raw fish and marinated rice — and I drink a small bottle of saki. Then I pull the blanket around me, after asking the stewardess not to wake me up for the meals or drinks, and especially not for the films. Then I fall into a deep sleep . . .

Akio Morita

TRAVELLING LIGHT

I made my first million from the front seat of a Model T Ford, which I had bought second hand. The car was my head office, and general headquarters for my work sites. It was sometimes even my hotel room.

John Paul Getty

TRIAL AND ERROR

The laboratory of a factory is the best place to learn about failure! Actually, all researchers worth their salt know that in the lab, 99 per cent of the people are working on lost causes. The modest percentage of success, nevertheless, serves to compensate for all the rest of the effort. Finally, I don't regret the thousands of times I came home empty-handed, having lost all my ammunition and bait. When the days get as gloomy as that, then you know you will soon find the treasure. And the flash of light, the sudden soaring hope, makes you forget all the difficult hours.

Soichiro Honda

TRICKERY

I know how, when necessary, to change the skin of the lion for that of the fox.

Napoleon

It is true that you can fool all the people some of the time; you can even fool some of the people all of the time; but you can't fool all of the people all of the time.

Abraham Lincoln

You can fool all of the people all of the time if the advertising is right, and the budget is big enough.

Joseph E. Levine

TRUST

When large amounts are at stake, it is preferable not to trust anyone.

Agatha Christie

We sell the trust a client must have in a salesman and in our company.

J. Michael Curto

I always believe someone's word until I have proof of the contrary, and I've concluded a great many profitable business deals with a simple handshake. On the other hand, I have also been sufficiently abused so that I've become a confirmed cynic.

Ray Kroc

TURNING BACK

No one can turn back, not successfully. One makes a decision to go forward, for better or worse, with the feeling and faith that if you succeed at one task, you have every reason to believe that you will succeed at your next, bigger one. There are no guarantees of course, but the risk must be taken, if you are going to live with yourself thereafter.

Harold Geneen

U

ULCERS

I don't have ulcers; I give them.

Harry Cohen

A doctor declares that many directors who complain of ulcers don't really have them. Suffering from ulcers has become a status symbol. There are certain types of executives who would rather die than admit they have no stomach pains. That would mean that they're just like everybody else!

Not being an authority on medicine, I cannot judge the matter. But I can have a good laugh in private, when I hear a 28- or 30-year-old executive who works 48 hours a week at most — minus the time he spends on lunch and golf — whimpering because he's overworked or that he's under terrible pressure. The real giants and geniuses of American business normally work 16 to 18 hours a day — often 7 days a week — and rarely take vacations. As a result, most of them live very long lives.

John Paul Getty

UNITY

My father, before giving us his blessing upon his final parting, reminded us that we should consider all men as brothers, according to the will of God; that after he departed, we should try to help men according to our means, with no distinction of faith or race. He exhorted us to remain firmly united and to continue working together on the operations of the bank he created.

He quoted a Scythian chieftain who, on his deathbed, called together all his sons and gave them each in turn a bunch of arrows, which none of them were able to break. Then, separating the bunch, he took the arrows one by one and broke them. 'As long as you remain united', he said, 'you will be strong. The day you separate will mark the end of your prosperity.'

James Rothschild

Jesus recognized that by living with the conscience of Christ, a person has no limitations. He turns his gaze towards God, source and creator of all, and thanks Him for always providing men with the force and substance necessary to satisfy all their needs. Thus He breaks bread and has it distributed by his disciples. And when everyone was served there were still twelve baskets left over. Jesus never counted on a neighbour's surplus to nourish Himself or others. He taught that our substances are part of the Universal Substance, where there is enough for all. We just have to exteriorize this substance to create anything we want.

Baird T. Spalding

URGENCY
See also Ambition.

I had talent. I wanted to be my own boss. I just had to.

Ralph Lauren

V

VALUE

Never underestimate yourself. You are the most important thing in your universe.

Edward L. Kramer

I am young, that's true, but for well-born souls, value does not depend on the number of years.

Pierre Corneille

VICTORY

I will return victorious or I will not return.

Ludovic Halevy

VIGILANCE

The man who is above his business may one day find his business above him.

Daniel Drew

VIRTUE

Virtue has its own rewards, but no sales at the box office.

Mae West

VISUALIZING

I saw in my mind hundreds of McDonald's restaurants in all corners of the land.

Ray Kroc

If in your mind's eye you see a successful venture, a deal made, a profit accomplished, it has a superb chance of actually happening. Projecting your mind into a successful situation is the most powerful means to achieve goals. If you spend time with pictures of failure in your mind, you will orchestrate failure.

Estée Lauder

VOCATION

Choose the kind of business which suits your temperament and taste. There are people who are purely mechanical. There are others for whom just the thought of machines is repellent. There lies the difference.

So, taking myself as an example, I would have never made a good negotiator. Neither could I ever be satisfied with a fixed salary; because my disposition is purely speculative, while so many others are just the opposite. Consequently, let each person be careful to choose the occupation that suits him best.

P.T. Barnum

W

WAR

Formerly when great fortunes were only made in war, war was a business; but now when great fortunes are only made by business, business is war.

Christian N. Bovee

In war you do not have to be nice — you only have to be right.

Winston Churchill

WASTE

I've always hated waste. When styles changed from narrow ties to wide ties, I put all my narrow ones aside for the day when they'd come back into fashion.

Lee Iacocca

WILLPOWER

Willpower can and should be considered a greater subject of pride than talent.

Honoré de Balzac

Precarious willpower is translated into words: strong willpower into actions.

Gustave Le Bon

WINNING

Winning isn't everything. But it's the only thing that counts.

Vince Lombardi

I do not think that winning is the most important thing. I think winning is the only thing.

Bill Veeck

WINNING FORMULAS
See also Key to Success.

Many people, young and old, have asked me from time to time for the secret of my success in business. Usually I avoided giving any answer. Now I can reveal it: the secret of how to succeed in business or in life is that there is no secret. No secret at all. No formula. No theory.

Harold Geneen

The chicken I served and which appeared on the menu was seasoned with herbs and spices; it was so superior to ordinary fried chicken, it was so delicious and satisfying, that I didn't dare add another ingredient to the recipe for fear of ruining a good thing, and alienating my clients who would not appreciate the change, and who would not come back to the restaurant afterwards.

Colonel Sanders

I would like to convince young businesspeople that a magic formula which is infallible and leads to sure success in business does not exist . . .that there is no automatic set of rules that will make a person a millionaire.

John Paul Getty

WISDOM
See also Knowlege; Learning from Others; Self-knowledge.

Knowing others is wisdom. Knowing yourself is superior wisdom.

Lao-Tzu

WOMEN
See also Men.

Whatever women do they must do twice as well as men to be thought half as good. Luckily this is not difficult.

Charlotte Whitton

There's an old saying, 'Never send a boy to do a man's job, send a lady'.

John Fitzgerald Kennedy

Most hierarchies were established by men who now monopolize the upper levels, thus depriving women of their rightful share of opportunities for incompetence.

Laurence J. Peter

WORK
See also Effort; Elbow Grease; Extra Mile; Laziness; Struggle.

If you are one of those who think that only arduous work and uncompromising honesty lead to success, then you'd better wisen up! Large fortunes are not made solely on hard work. They are the results of meeting precise demands, based on the application of certain laws, and not on chance or luck.

Napoleon Hill

There is no substitute for hard work.

Thomas A. Edison

Work is indispensable to man's happiness: it elevates and consoles, irrespective of the kind of work as long as it benefits someone. Doing what you can is doing what you should.

Alexander Dumas the Younger

Work is nourishment for noble souls.

Seneca

Wherever a man works, he leaves something of his soul.

Henryk Sienkiewicz

No one can get very far in life by being satisfied with working 40 hours a week.

Bill Marriot

It was not as difficult as it seemed. Actually, all I had to do was work nonstop.

Robert Woodruff

For years, I was content to eat, sleep and work. And now, all my friends are still at work, and I'm having a good time.

Ron Rice

If people knew how hard I worked to acquire this talent, they would no longer be surprised.

Michelangelo

With willpower, ideas, and a willingness to work two hours longer than others, it is not difficult to make money.

Bernard Brochard

Most people are surprised by the way I work. I play it very loose. I don't carry a briefcase. I try not to schedule too many meetings. I leave my door open. You can't be imaginative or entrepreneurial if you've got too much structure. I prefer to come to work each day and just see what develops.

Donald Trump

Choose a job that you like, and you will not have to work a day of your life.

Confucius

Life is work, and everything you undertake adds to your experience.

Henry Ford

The average man dedicates 25 per cent of his energy to work. The world rewards the person who gives more than 50 per cent, and does anything for those rare individuals who give 100 per cent.

Andrew Carnegie

The desire to work is so rare that is must be encouraged wherever it is found.

Abraham Lincoln

I never did anything worth doing by accident, nor did any of my inventions come by accident; they came by work.

Thomas A. Edison

WORKAHOLICS

You start by wanting money. Then you get swept away by the love of work.

Coco Chanel

People who work a lot do not work hard.

Henry David Thoreau

I have never met a man who works seven days a week who has not been physically or mentally ill.

Sir Robert Peel

Those who are skilled in archery bend their bow only when they are preparing to use it; when they do not require it, they allow it to remain unbent, for otherwise it would be unserviceable when the time for using it arrived. So it is with man. If he were to devote himself unceasingly to a dull round of business, without breaking the monotony by cheerful amusements, he would fall imperceptibly into idiocy, or be struck by paralysis. It is the conviction of this truth that leads to the proper division of my time.

Herodotus

252 · WORKING FOR YOURSELF

WORKING FOR YOURSELF

Being in your own business is working 80 hours a week so that you can avoid working 40 hours a week for someone else.

Ramona E.F. Arnett

I worked and worked. Although days only have 24 hours, I worked 50! Imagine, not only did I prepare my creams by hand, I also put them in pots, stuck on the labels — and then sold them. I did the publicity, I went from store to store with my products. At that time, pharmacies were the only outlets. I went to six in a week, eight the next week. Luckily, I wasn't lacking for energy.

Helena Rubinstein

When people saw me working in the laboratory, some would say that the commander is wearing his field uniform. However, God knows I never went to the lab with a tragic or military attitude. I went for the simple reason that I enjoy working, and it isn't because I'm president that I would deprive myself of that pleasure! Why should a man, just because he is the director of a company, spend his days seated behind a desk, twiddling his thumbs to pass the time? Of course, there are other ways to keep busy, I don't want to be difficult, and I accept the fact that other directors are more interested in numbers and charts than in getting their hands dirty in the workshop. But there it is . . . it would be hard for an engineer like myself to enjoy accounting, especially when we have highly skilled experts to do it for us. I assume that being president is not a punishment. If it were, I'm sure one of my faithful friends would have warned me!

Soichiro Honda

It's not how many hours you put in, it's what you get done while you're working.

Donald Trump

WORRY
See also Pressure; Problems.

The reason why worry kills more people than work is that more people worry than work.

Robert Frost

Businessmen who cannot combat their worries die young.

Dr Alexis Carrel

It is not work that kills men; it is worry. Work is healthy; you can hardly put more upon a man than he can bear. Worry is rust upon the blade. It is not the revolution that destroys the machinery, but the friction.

Henry Ward Beecher

It's when business is too good that I get worried, thinking the situation will take a sudden turn for the worse.

Walt Disney

I learned at that time how to avoid getting crushed by problems. I refused to worry about more than one thing at a time, and I didn't allow myself to be needlessly tormented by a useless problem, however important it was, to the point of not being able to sleep. This is more easily said than done. I did it by using my own technique of self-hypnosis. It's very possible that I read it somewhere in a book on the subject, I don't recall, but in any case I developed a system which allowed me to avoid all nervous tension and exclude my thoughts when I went to bed.

I knew that if I didn't do this, the next morning I would not be fresh and ready to deal with my clients. I saw my brain as a blackboard covered with messages, most of them urgent, and I practised imagining one hand with a cloth in it, erasing the blackboard. I emptied my brain completely. When a thought began to appear, I wiped it away! I erased it before it had time to form. Then I relaxed my entire body, starting with the neck, down through the shoulders, arms, torso, legs, right to the toes. And in this way I could go to sleep. People were amazed to see me working 12 to 14 hours a day during some animated convention, and then go out at night and party 'til the early hours; and the next morning appear fresh and relaxed, ready to see my clients.

Ray Kroc

WRITING

The discipline you use to write things down clearly is the first step in making them real.

Lee Iacocca

Y

YACHTS

Any man who has to worry about the annual upkeep of his yacht can't afford to own one.

J.P. Morgan

YOUTH

It is an extremely arduous, difficult and boring process. I practically camped outside the doors of a number of company directors before they gave me the chance to do something. It's very simple; I was much too young, and they didn't believe in youth at Universal. Well, not anymore!

Steven Spielberg

It takes a long time to become young.

Pablo Picasso

Z

ZEAL
See also Ardour; Enthusiasm.

Do you know anyone who is zealous in their work? He is the equal of kings.

John Rockefeller

Appendix

A

Adams, Joey, American comedian and journalist

Alain, French philosopher and essayist

Allaire, Paul A., President of Xerox

Allen, Fred, President, Pitney Bowes Company

Allen, Woody, American film actor, writer and director

Amoss, Lisa M., Professor, School of Business, Tulane University

Aristophanes, Greek comic poet

Aristotle, Greek philosopher

Armstrong, Neil, American astronaut, first man on the moon

Arnett, Ramona E.F., President of Ramona Enterprises

Ash, Mary Kay, Founder and President of Mary Kay Cosmetics

Augustus Caesar, Roman Emperor

Aweida, Jesse, President, Storage Technology

Aymé, Marcel, French writer

B

Bacon, Francis, 16th-century English statesman and philosopher

Balzac, Honoré de, 19th-century French writer

Banville, Théodore de, 19th-century French poet

Barclay, Eddie, French film producer

Barnum, P.T., 19th-century American entertainment entrepreneur

Barrymore, John, American actor

Bata, Thomas, largest shoe manufacturer in the world

Beaverbrook, Lord, British (Canadian-born) newspaper publisher

Beecher, Henry Ward, 19th-century American preacher and lecturer

Behan, Brendan, Irish dramatist

Benetton, Annette, President of Benetton France

Benn, Stanley I., Management writer and consultant

Bennis, Warren G., President, University of Cincinnati

Benny, Jack, American comedian

Bergen, Edgar, Radio personality and ventriloquist

Bergson, Henri, French Nobel laureate in literature

Berle, Milton, American comedian

Berlin, Irving, American (Russian-born) popular composer

Bettencourt, Lilliane, The richest woman in France, daughter of the founder of L'Oréal

Bich, Marcel, Inventor of the ball-point pen

Biderman, Maurice, Number-one French retailer of men's clothes

Bismarck, Otto von, 19th-century politician; first Chancellor of the German Empire 1871—1890

Blenstein-Blanchet, Marcel, Founder of the Publicis Agency (France)

Bloch, Arthur, writer and humourist

Block, Henry, H&R Block

Blumkin, Rose, Founder of Omaha Nebraska Furniture Mart

Bohr, Niels, Danish physicist, Nobel Laureate

Boileau-Despréaux, Nicolas, 17th-century French critic and poet

Bonaparte, Napoleon, Emperor of France 1804—1815

Borch, Fred J., General Electric

Bourg, Claude, Businesswoman, Director of a temporary employment agency

Bovee, Christian N., 19th-century Author and editor

Braddock, Richard, Vice-president of Citicorp

Brandeis, Louis D., Former U.S. Supreme Court Justice

Bresman, William J., President of Cable Division: Teleprompter Corporation

Brochard, Bernard, President of Havas Eurocom Advertising Agency

Brooks, Joseph E., Lord & Taylor

Brower, Charles, President, Batton, Barton, Durstine & Osborn

Bruyère, Jean de la, 17th-century French moralist

Bucy, J. Fred, Texas Instruments

Buffon, Comte Georges-Louis Leclerc de, 18th-century French naturalist and writer

Burke, Jim, President, Johnson & Johnson

Burns, H.S.M., Former President, Shell Oil & Company

Burr, Donald, Founder, PeopleExpress Airlines

Burton, Richard, British actor

Bushnell, Nolan, Founder of Atari Computer Company

Butler, Nicholas Murray, American educator and Nobel Laureate

Butler, Samuel, 19th-century British novelist

Byrne, John J., Geico Corporation

Byrom, Fletcher, President of de Koppers

C

Caillois, Roger, French writer and philosopher

Camus, Albert, French philosopher and writer

Cantor, Eddie, American singer, comedian and writer

Carlson, Ed, Former President of United Airlines

Carnegie, Andrew, 19th-century American industrialist and philanthropist

Carnegie, Dale, American orator

Carrel, Dr Alexis, French surgeon and biologist

Carter, Shelby H. Jr, President of Xerox Information Systems Group

Castiglione, Baldassare, 15th-century Italian statesman and author

Caesar, Julius, Roman general and emperor

Chanel, Coco, French fashion designer

Chaplin, Charlie, American (British-born) author, actor and film director

Chesterfield, Philip Dormer Stanhope, Lord, 18th-century British writer, statesman, diplomat, orator and journalist

Chesterton, G.K., British poet, essayist and critic

Christie, Dame Agatha, British novelist

Churchill, Winston, British statesman; Prime Minister 1940—1945 and 1951—1955

Cicero, Roman politician and orator

Cocteau, Jean, French writer and filmmaker

Cohen, Harry, American film producer

Coleman, George, 18th-/19th-century British dramatic author

Confucius, Chinese philosopher

Conrad, Joseph, British (Polish-born) novelist

Constant de Rebeque, Benjamin, 18th-/ 19th-century French politican and writer

Corneille, Pierre, 17th-century French dramatic poet

Crockett, David, 18th-/19th-century American pioneer and soldier

Curto, J. Michael, Vice-president, U.S. Steel Corporation

D

Dassault, Marcel, French aviator

David-Neel, Alexandra, Franco-British writer

Davidson, Jeffrey P., Marketing consultant

Debussy, Claude, 19th-century French composer

Defoe, Daniel, 17th-/18th-century British novelist, poet and journalist

de Gaulle, Charles, French general and statesman

De Kooning, Willem, American (Dutch-born) painter

Demosthenes, Athenian orator and statesman

Descartes, René, 17th-century French philosopher and scholar

Destouche, Philippe, 17th-century, French dramatic author

Dickens, Charles, 19th-century British novelist

Diderot, Denis, 18th-century French writer and philosopher

Dior, Christian, French couturier

Disney, Walt, Hungarian-born American animated film producer and director

Disraeli, Benjamin, 19th-century British politician, Prime Minister 1868 and 1874—1880

Dostoïevski, Fiodor, 19th-century Russian novelist

Doyle, Sir Arthur Conan, British novelist and dramatic writer

Drucker, Peter, Management consultant

Duke, J.B., Founder of the American Tobacco Company

Dumas, Alexander *fils*, 19th-century French writer

Duncan, Joseph W., Chief statistician, Dun & Bradstreet Corporation

Du Pont de Nemours, Pierre Samuel, American financier

Durocher, Leo, American baseball player and manager

Dutourd, Jean, French novelist

Dylan, Bob, American singer and songwriter

E

Edison, Thomas A., American inventor of the telegraph and the electric lightbulb

Einstein, Albert, American (German-born) physicist

Eisenhower, Dwight David, 34th President of the United States

Emerson, Charles Knight d', Chairman, Emerson Electric

Emerson, Ralph Waldo, 19th-century American poet and essayist

Epictetus, Stoic philosopher

Erasmus, 15th-/16th-century Dutch humanist

Esber, Edward M., President of Ashton-Tate

Euripides, Greek tragic poet

F

Fielding, Henry, 18th-century British novelist, journalist, dramatist and poet

Fitzgerald, F. Scott, American novelist

Foch, Ferdinand, French politician

Forbes, Malcolm, Editor-in-Chief of *Forbes Magazine*

Ford, Charlotte, member of the Ford family; manager of the Ford Foundation

Ford, Henry, American industrialist, pioneer of the automobile

Ford, Henry II, grandson of Henry Ford

Franklin, Benjamin, 18th-century American politician, writer and inventor

Friedman, Milton, American economist

Frost, Robert, American poet

Fuller, Thomas, 17th-century British author

G

Galbraith, John Kenneth, American (Canadian-born) economist and diplomat

Gandhi, Mahatma (Mohandas), Indian philosopher and statesman

Garaudy, Roger, French scholar and politician

Garfield, James Abram, 19th-century American politician; 20th President of the United States

Geneen, Harold, President, AT & T

Getty, John Paul, Former President of Getty Oil Company

Gibbon, Edward, 18th-century British historian

Gide, André, French writer

Girard, Joe, American car salesman; highly sucessful in the 1970s

Godefroy, Christian, Founder and President of Godefroy Publications (French mail-order book firm)

Goethe, 18-/19th-century German poet and dramatist

Goizueta, Robert, President of Coca-Cola

Goldsmith, Sir James, Franco-British financier

Goldwyn, Samuel, American (Polish-born) pioneer of the Hollywood film industry

Goncourt, Edmond, 19th-century French historian and writer

Gordy, Berry, Founder of Motown Records

Gracian, Baltazar, 17th-century Spanish moralist and essayist

Grant, Albert A., President of the American Civil Engineers Association

Guitry, Lucien, 19th-century French actor

Guitry, Sacha, French actor and dramatist

Guizot, Francois, 19th-century French politician and historian

Gyllenhammar, Pehr G., President of Volvo

H

Halévy, Ludovic, 19th-century French writer

Half, Robert, President of Robert Half International

Haliburton, Thomas, 19th-century Canadian jurist and humourist

Hall, Joyce Clyde, Founder of Hallmark Cards Inc

Hanley, John, President of Monsanto

Hannibal, Carthaginian general and statesman

Hansen, Robert, President of Deere

Harness, Edward G., Former President of Proctor and Gamble

Hatsopoulos, Georges, Founder of Thermo Electron

Hazlitt, William, 19th-century, British essayist

Head, Howard, Inventor of the Head metal ski

Hearst, William Randolph, American newspaper publisher

Hegel, Friedrich, 19th-century German philosopher

Héliand, Tasle d', French philosopher

Heraclitus, Greek philosopher

Herodotus, Greek historian

Hersant, Robert, French journalist and founder, Hersant Press Group

Herzog, Raymond, Former President of 3M Company

Hill, Napoleon, American author

Hilton, Conrad, Founder of the Hilton Hotel chain

Hoglend, Ron, President of Sherwood's Commercial Brokers

Honda, Soichiro, Founder of the Honda Motor Company

Hook, Harold S., CEO: American General Corporation

Horace, Roman poet

Hsieh, Tehyi, Chinese educator, writer and diplomat

Hubbard, Elbert, American writer, publisher and editor

Hubbard, Frank McKinney, American cartoonist and humourist

Hughes, Howard, American businessman; founder of Hughes Tool Company

Hugo, Victor, 19th-century French writer

I

Iacocca, Lee, CEO, Chrysler Corporation

Ibsen, Henrik, 19th-century Norwegian poet and dramatist

Ishihara, Takashi, President of Nissan

J

Jackson, Holbrook, British writer and editor

James, William, late 19th-century American psychologist

Jefferson, Thomas, 18th-/19th-century American politician; 3rd President of the United States

Jobs, Steven, Co-founder of Apple Computers

Johnson, General, Founder of Johnson & Johnson

Johnson, John H., Director of Ebony

Johnson, Lyndon Baines, American politician; 36th President of the United States

Johnson, Robert W., Johnson & Johnson

Johnson, Samuel, 18th-century British writer, dramatist and lexicographer

Johnson, Samuel C., President of S.C. Johnson & Son Inc.

Johnston, Eric, Former President, U.S. Chamber of Commerce

Jones, Arthur, Founder of Nautilus Sports-Medical Industries

Jones, Reginald H., General Electric

Joubert, Joseph, 18th-/19th century French moralist and critic

K

Kaiser, Henry J., American industrialist

Kant, Immanuel, 18th-century German philosopher

Kennedy, John Fitzgerald, 35th President of the United States

Kennedy, Joseph, Father of John F. Kennedy, U.S. ambassador to England

Kennedy, Rose, Kennedy family matriarch

Keoch, Donald E., President of Coca-Cola

Kerkorian, Kirk, Metro-Goldwyn-Mayer

Kettering, Charles F., President of GM Research Corporation

Keynes, John Maynard, British economist, writer and diplomat

Kiam, Victor, President, Remington

King, Martin Luther Jr, American Civil Rights activist, Baptist preacher, winner of the Nobel Peace Prize in 1964

Kipling, Rudyard, British poet and novelist

Kissinger, Henry, American politician and statesman

Knopf, Alfred, publisher

Knudsen, William, Ford Motor Company

Koch, Ed, Former Mayor of New York City

Koch, James, President, The Boston Beer Company

Korda, Michael, Editor-in-Chief of Simon & Schuster

Kroc, Ray, Founder of McDonalds

L

Lagardère, Jean-Luc, Matra Corporation

Land, Edwin H., Founder of Polaroid

Landers, Ann, American advice columnist

Lao-Tzu, Chinese philosopher, founder of Taoism

Larsen, Edna, Avon sales representative

Lauder, Estée, Founder, Estée Lauder Cosmetics

Lauren, Ralph, Founder, Ralph Lauren Clothes

Lawrence, T.E., British soldier, archaeologist and writer

Layard, Austen Henry, 19th-century British archaeologist and diplomat

Leacock, Stephen, Canadian humourist

Le Bon, Gustave, French doctor and sociologist

Lebowitz, Fran, American author and comedian

LeFevre, William M. Jr, Granger & Company

Lehr, Lew, President of 3M

Lennon, John, British composer, singer and artist

Levi-Montalcini, Rita, Winner of the Nobel Prize in Physiology

Levine, Joseph E., American show business producer

Levitt, Theodore, Editor of the Harvard Business Review

Lie, Trygve Halvdan, Former Secretary General of the United Nations

Lincoln, Abraham, 16th President of the United States

Little, Royal, Founder of Textron

Lloyd George, David, British Prime Minister 1916—1922

Lombardi, Vince, Former Coach of the New York Giants football team

Louis XIV, King of France 1643—1715

M

McCarthy, Charlie.

Newman, Wallace 'Chief', Whittier
College football coach
Newton, Isaac, 17th-century British
mathematician, physician,
astronomer and thinker
Nietzsche, Friedrich, 19th-century
German philosopher

O

Ogilvy, David, Co-founder, Ogilvy
and Mather Advertising Agency
Onassis, Aristotle, Greek shipping
magnate and businessman
Ou-Tse, Chinese philosopher

P

Packard, David, Co-founder,
Hewlett-Packard
Parkinson, C. Northcote, Author of
The Peter Principle
Pascal, Blaise, 17th-century French
scientist and philosopher
Pascale, Richard T., Stanford
University School of Business
Pasteur, Louis, 19th-century French
chemist and biologist, discoverer
of microbiology
Pauling, Linus, American chemist,
winner of the Nobel Prize for
Chemistry
Pauwels, Louis, Co-author (with
Jacques Bergier) of *Morning Of
The Magicians*
Pearson, Andy, President of PepsiCo
Peel, Sir Robert, 19th-century British
politician
Peers, John, President of Logical
Machine Corporation
Perot, H. Ross, Founder of
Electronic Data Systems
Peter, Laurence J., University of
Southern California
Peters, Thomas, Co-author (with

Robert Waterman) of *In Search of
Excellence*
Peterson, Peter, Former President,
Bell & Howell
Picasso, Pablo, Spanish painter and
sculptor
Plato, Greek philosopher
Player, Gary, British (South African-
born) Professional golfer
Pompidou, Georges, French
politician; Premier 1962—1968,
President 1969—1974
Port, Rich, President of Rich Port
Realties Agency
Poussin, Nicolas, 17th-century
French painter
Pou-Tché, Tch'ao, Chinese
philosopher
Presley, Elvis, American singer
Publilius Syrus, Roman author

Q

Quadracci, Henry V., President of
Quad Graphics Inc.

R

Racine, Jean, 17th-century French
dramatic poet
Raleigh, Sir Walter, 16th-century
British navigator, writer and
nobleman
Rand, Ayn, American author
Rathenau, Walther, German
politician
Reagan, Ronald, 40th President of
the United States
Redford, Robert, American actor
and director
Régine, Nightclub magnate
Renan, Ernest, French writer
Renard, Jules, 19th-century French
writer

Revson, Charles, Founder of Revlon Inc.

Ricard, Paul, Producer of Ricard Liquor

Rice, Ron, Founder of Tanning Research Laboratories

Riklis, Meshulam, President of Rapid American Corporation

Robbins, Irvine, Co-Founder of Baskin-Robbins Ice-Cream

Rochefoucauld, Duc de la, 17th-century French moralist and writer

Rockefeller, John, American industrialist and financier, Founder of Standard Oil

Rockefeller, Nelson, American statesman

Rockne, Knute, American (Norwegian-born) sportsman and football coach

Rodgers, Francis G., Vice-president of Marketing for IBM

Rogers, Will, American actor and humourist

Rolland, Romain, French writer

Roosevelt, Eleanor, American stateswoman and humanitarian

Roosevelt, Franklin, 32nd President of the United States

Roosevelt, Theodore, 26th President of the United States

Rostand, Jean, French biologist and author

Rothschild, Guy de, Great-grandson of James, Founder of the Rothschild Bank (France)

Rothschild, James, 19th-century Parisian financier and banker

Rousseau, Jean-Jacques, 18th-century Franco-Swiss writer and philosopher

Rubinstein, Helena, Founder of the cosmetics empire, formerly one of the richest women in the world

Ruskin, John, 19th-century British essayist, critic and reformer

Russell, Bertrand, British mathematician, logician and philosopher

S

Sadat, Anwar, Former President of Egypt

Sagan, Francoise, French writer

Saint-Exupéry, Antoine de, French writer and aviator

Sanders, Colonel, Founder of Kentucky Fried Chicken

Santayana, George, American (Spanish-born) poet and philosopher

Sarnoff, David, Founder and President of RCA

Sassoon, Vidal, British hairstylist

Savile, George, 17th-century British politician and statesman

Schultz, George, U.S. Secretary of State

Schultz, Peter, President and CEO of Porsche

Schwab, Charles, First President of United States Steel Company

Schweitzer, Albert, French theologian, philosopher, musician, doctor and missionary

Seitz, Nick, Sports commentator, editor of Golf Digest

Selye, Hans, Canadian (Austrian-born) physiologist

Seneca, Roman politican, writer and philosopher

Setton, Jacky, President of Pioneer-France

Sévigné, Madame de, 17th-century French writer

Shakespeare, William, 16th-century British poet and dramatist

Shaw, George Bernard, British author and dramatist

Walters, Vernon, U.S. statesman

Walton, Sam, Founder and President
of Wal-Mart

Wanamaker, John, Founder of
Wanamaker's Department Stores

Wang, An, Founder and CEO, Wang
Laboratories

Ward, Lewis Bookwalter, Harvard
Business School

Waterman, Robert, Management
consultant and writer; co-author
(with Thomas Peters) of *In Search
of Excellence*

Watson, Thomas J. Sr, Founder and
first President of IBM

Webb, James L., First administrator
of NASA

Webster, Daniel, 19th-century
American statesman and orator

Weil, André, French mathematician

Wiesenfeld, Paul R., American
attorney

Weizmann, Chaïm, Israeli
statesman

Wellington, Duke of, 18th-/19th-
century British General and
politician

West, Mae, American actress, singer
and comedian

Whitehead, Alfred North, American
philosopher

Whitton, Charlotte, Former Mayor of
the city of Ottawa (Canada)

Wilde, Oscar, 19th-century British
author and dramatist

Williams, William Carlos, American
poet, novelist and essayist

Wilson, Earl, Syndicated columnist

Wood, General Robert, Former
President of Sears

Woodruff, Robert, Former President
of Coca-Cola

Wrapp, M. Edward, Professor of
Business Management at the
University of Chicago

Wrigley, William (1861—1932),
Founder and President, Wrigley &
Company

Wriston, Walter, President of
Citicorp

X

Xiaoping, Deng, Chinese politician

Y

Yamasaki, Yoshiki, Mazda

Young, John, Hewlett-Packard

Young, Owen D. (1874—1962),
General Electric

Yutang, Lin (1895—1976), Chinese
philosopher and author

Z

Zalisnick, Abraham, Business
psychologist

Index